Flying Scotsman

This book is dedicated to Flying Scotsman's *designers, crew, owners and supporters, past, present and future. They have wrought miracles, and continue to do so.*

FLYING
SCOTSMAN

The Extraordinary Story of the
World's Most Famous Train

ANDREW RODEN

First published in Great Britain
2007 by Aurum Press Limited
7 Greenland Street
London NW1 0ND

A catalogue record for this book is available from the British Library.

ISBN-10: 1 84513 241 6
ISBN-13: 978 1 84513 241 5

3 5 7 9 10 8 6 4 2
2007 2009 2011 2010 2008

Typeset by SX Composing DTP, Rayleigh, Essex
Printed and bound in Great Britain by MPG Books, Bodmin

Contents

Preface

In the early-1950s, *Flying Scotsman*, the world's most famous steam locomotive, was sent from her old stamping grounds on the line north from King's Cross to help haul passenger trains from Leicester to London Marylebone on the old Great Central line.

One day, she was rostered to take over the Sheffield to Marylebone 'South Yorkshire Pullman' from Leicester to the capital. It was a fairly routine duty, and although an extra couple of coaches had been added as it was a public holiday, it was well within the capabilities of this Brunswick-green racehorse.

Problems had been reported with *Flying Scotsman*'s injectors the day before, but by the time the young fireman, Ken Issitt, joined the locomotive at the Leicester shed they had been resolved.

The Gresley-designed locomotive rapidly gathered pace on her way south from Leicester, getting to grips with her load, and cantering down the flat and level Great Central Main Line. Soon after it passed Charwelton in Northamptonshire, however, the right-hand injector began to leak water, a sure sign that something was awry. *Flying Scotsman* would normally have been able to keep pace with the steaming rate on just one injector, but Issitt kept having to supplement it with short bursts from the left-hand injector. Things got worse, and the right-hand injector failed completely just after the train went past Aylesbury. Although this wasn't dangerous, it meant that Issitt and Cyril Chamberlain, the driver, would have to work hard to conserve steam in order to avoid draining the boiler.

The situation worsened further. The left-hand – and hitherto reliable – injector started playing up. Issitt tried everything he could think of to get it working, but as the train passed Wendover, near Aylesbury, that too failed. With no way of getting water into the boiler, things were looking serious. By now, Issitt had stopped firing, but the burning coals in the firebox would boil all the water away, and that could lead to only one thing: a catastrophic boiler explosion. Drastic action was called for.

'The fire had to come out pretty damn quick,' recalls Issitt. 'Bear in mind that there's something like 41 square feet of grate area in the firebox and at least two tonnes of burning coal in there, and you can see the problem we had.

'I began winding the grate down while Cyril struggled with the injector. He set the engine coasting with the regulator barely open.'

Issitt took the long fire shovel from the tender and started pushing the fire from the firebox into the ashpan. As *Flying Scotsman* continued running, burning coals showered from her underside as if she was bleeding. The vegetation on the embankments and cuttings – despite being well tended – was soon ablaze.

The two men were doing everything within their power,

and Issitt pushed himself to the limits of exhaustion frantically trying to remove the heat source from the boiler in order to save their locomotive and the passengers on the train.

'The fire shovel was beginning to become soft and bend with the heat. The water level had disappeared in the glass. We looked anxiously into the firebox to see if the lead plugs in its roof had melted, and for the telltale hiss of steam telling us how near we were to disaster and the need for us to run for our lives. We were seconds away from oblivion.'

Unless Chamberlain could get the injectors working and get water into the boiler, the lead plugs in the firebox roof would, as Issitt points out, melt, venting steam into the firebox to warn the crew of danger and relieve the increasingly explosive pressure. However, this would be no solution – merely a way of buying the crew a few precious extra seconds. After the lead plugs had melted, the water would fall below the copper surface of the inner firebox, which ordinarily was kept from melting only by the water that surrounded it absorbing the heat. If the firebox had started to melt, the boiler would have been completely out of control. Anything could happened – it could have imploded, sending the white-hot steam back into the cab and the train; it could have exploded, sending the boiler flying off *Flying Scotsman's* chassis; or any one of a number of other catastrophes could have wrecked the engine. The only certainty is that Issitt and Chamberlain – and many of their passengers – would have been killed or seriously injured.

With the train now coasting at 40mph, Chamberlain

continued to hammer, kick, coax and curse the injectors. There seemed nothing wrong with them. He and Issitt needed a miracle.

They got one: suddenly the injectors started to pick up water and send it into the boiler. There was no rhyme or reason for it, but Chamberlain wasn't going to worry about that for the moment. He shouted across to his mate: 'I've got it working!'

'Thank God,' said a relieved Issitt.

Flying Scotsman was nursed to London, arriving just five minutes late. She was clearly not in a fit state to return to Leicester until the problem had been sorted once and for all. Issitt was sufficiently intrigued by the day's difficulties to find out what had caused them. 'There was nothing wrong with the injectors. They separated the engine from the tender for inspection and found algae and rust had blocked the strainers in the tender.

'When the fitters drained the tender, they found three buckets of live fish – roach, bream, rudd – all swimming around happily, living off the algae in the tender!'

It may sound like a fishy tale, but the Leicester shed took its water from a canal through a nine-inch pipe. The fish had been sucked up through this and sent straight into *Flying Scotsman's* tender, where they happily feasted on the algae. They could never have known just how close they came to destroying a national icon.

On another day, Issitt and Chamberlain would rightly have been acclaimed as heroes, but for them, all that lay ahead now was a trip back to Leicester behind a lesser engine. If ever a steam locomotive was to prove the cat with nine lives of the railways, it was *Flying Scotsman*. She had just used up her first. The following fifty years would see her need all the others.

Chapter One
Starting Lines

January 1963 was cold. Temperatures fell to -16° C, the River Thames froze over, and even the sea froze in Herne Bay. Even if Cliff Richard was doing his best to cheer up shivering Britain with 'Bachelor Boy' at number one, it wasn't a promising start to a momentous year that would eventually see the Beatles release their first album and President Kennedy assassinated.

Moreover, King's Cross had always been one of London's less exciting stations, lacking the glamour of international movie stars and heads of state arriving and departing, and without the cheery bustle of summer hordes going on their holidays. It exuded a much grittier atmosphere, rooted firmly in the hinterlands of the English Midlands, of Yorkshire and Northumberland, and of the Scottish Lowlands, from where much of its business came. In part this was down to the looming portals of Gasworks Tunnel, sentinel on the station's northern approaches, through whose smoke and brimstone commuters, businessmen, tourists and politicians all ventured in and out of the capital.

On 14 January 1963, in a filthy, soot-encrusted shed just a few hundred yards away, near York Way, a working-class man stood back from his charge. It had taken huge effort, but after hours of patient and determined work, she was ready.

Her big black nose shone in the weak, early morning sunlight, and her steel limbs glistened with a sheen of lubricating oil and paraffin just a few molecules thick. From perhaps six feet above the man's head came the sound of steel on steel, followed by the grating of cold, polished shovel against frozen, unwilling coal. A quick shuffle of feet, then a clang as the bottom of the shovel's blade bounced off an iron casting protecting vital copper, propelling its contents eleven feet forward to land on a precisely selected patch of gently burning coal.

The man walked to his right, savouring, for the last time, the huge sweep of giant wheels that had propelled this beast at 100mph and made her the fastest in the world for a while: wheels that had been the first to run the 393 miles non-stop from London to Edinburgh, claiming another record in the process. Looming over the wheels, like a thoroughbred's body over its legs, was a giant Brunswick green-painted boiler. In its day this had been among the most advanced in the world, and even now, there was little to match it for sustained high-power output. Halfway along the beast's length, gently describing an arc over the middle set of big wheels, was the cast-brass nameplate, the letters equally spaced along its length – the most recognised name anywhere in the world: *Flying Scotsman*.

Flying Scotsman was no stranger to the history books, thanks to her glory days at the Wembley Exhibition in 1924, and two spectacular record-breaking runs in the 1920s and 1930s. She was as close as the railway could get to a national icon: a name recognised by millions, a name whose romance and speed summed up the age of steam. That age was almost over.

But not quite. Today was to be *Flying Scotsman*'s last in front-line service. Her career of forty years had come to a close, not because she was incapable of the work demanded of her – far from it: recent developments initiated at her King's Cross home, known as 'Top Shed', had made her one of the most efficient locomotives in the world. Instead, a faceless bureaucrat had decreed that she and her kin stood in the way of progress and must be replaced by the latest products from the white-hot blast furnace of technology. Never mind that the diesel locomotives that would replace her were unreliable, expensive and little more powerful: this was Progress, and that was all there was to it.

Standing next to the locomotive, shivering in the cold, was a former dive-bomber pilot in his early forties. Tall and well-built, with perhaps a little middle-age spread, he had a neatly trimmed moustache, and, though his hair was thinning, he nonetheless carried himself with the assurance and poise derived from extreme wealth. He was a member of the British Railways area board responsible for King's Cross, and he had risked his career to save this iconic locomotive from the scrap man's torch. He'd paid a princely sum for the privilege, and he still wasn't quite sure what he was going to do with this giant steam locomotive – but what he did know was that the nation would mourn her passing if nobody had stepped in to save her. By the end of *Flying Scotsman*'s journey to Doncaster that day (where she would be taken off the train and replaced by one of her slightly less glamorous sisters for the final leg to Leeds), Alan Pegler would own this locomotive: the first private individual in Britain ever to possess a front-line express steam locomotive in his own right.

Not surprisingly, Pegler was a popular character with the newsreel and television crews shivering with him at Top Shed. He was a swashbuckling, buccaneering character with a posh accent and slightly raffish demeanour. Why, they asked, had he bought his own steam locomotive? The insinuation that this was merely the whim of a man with money to burn was clear. Pegler was equally clear: he'd not saved *Flying Scotsman* for himself: he'd saved her for the nation, as the nation was unwilling to do so itself. He couldn't, he said, let this wonderful machine be scrapped.

Time ticked towards the Leeds-bound train's departure time of 1315, and like mourners at a wake, people from all over London and beyond came to pay their respects. It started as a trickle, then became a stream and then a torrent. Every vantage point at King's Cross was packed with people who ordinarily couldn't care less about railways, all wanting to see this momentous occasion: *Flying Scotsman*'s last departure from the station that she had been running to for almost all her career.

Flying Scotsman pulled away from Top Shed with Pegler on the footplate. Once on the main line, she reversed back into King's Cross station to be coupled to her train. As first the screw coupling linked locomotive with train, then the vital train brake pipe and finally the equally vital steam heat pipes were attached, anticipation reached a climax. Pegler stood on the front buffer beam to acknowledge the crowds who had come to see the locomotive that would soon be his. He stood with restrained dignity, doubtless glad of the warming heat of *Flying Scotsman*'s smokebox on his back. Before long, the guard was ready to whistle the train's departure to Leeds and Pegler hurried to the footplate. At the shrill of the guard's whistle, the driver opened the cylinder drain cocks, then the regulator slightly, before releasing the brakes. After a moment the high-pressure steam reached *Flying Scotsman*'s gigantic cylinders, and she inched forward, her great wheels sweeping round faster and faster as she got to grips with her heavy load.

The crowds waved their hats and cheered as the train pulled away from the platform and watched as she entered Gasworks Tunnel for the last time on her way north. They waited until the train's tail light had disappeared in the gloom and the distinctive sound of this three-cylinder locomotive had faded into the hustle and bustle of the city. This really did feel like the end of a golden age for those lucky enough to witness it.

Ever since then, *Flying Scotsman* has proved an enduring icon of the steam railway, the most popular locomotive in the world, the one which, if you ask somebody with no interest in railways to name a steam engine, they will name. She's become such a recognised name that it's now almost impossible to have a rational discussion about railway history, and particularly steam locomotive history, without her looming large – and this is something I've always questioned. I'm not old enough to have seen the glory days of the 1920s and 1930s, or the brief renaissance of the 1950s, or the sad decline of the 1960s – but even the most cursory look around the National Railway Museum in York (perhaps the greatest of all our national museums) proves that there were faster, more powerful, and more modern steam locomotives than *Flying Scotsman*. Why has she become known as a great locomotive when others, such as her speed-record-holding cousin *Mallard*, surely deserve many more plaudits?

Perhaps it's that *Flying Scotsman* so effortlessly embraces the old and the modern: nobody would ever mistake her for anything other than a steam locomotive, yet in her cleanliness of line and unfussy design, she looks modern. Perhaps her greatest achievement is that she paved the way for other designs to set new standards in power, speed and reliability. She arrived too late to dominate the great 'Races to the North', and too soon for the locomotive arms races of the 1930s; without her, though, advances such as non-stop long-distance trains and high-speed, lightweight flyers might not have happened. The tale of how *Flying Scotsman* came to be, and how she came to be so universally recognised and adored is one of human ingenuity and brilliance, of scheming politics, and of how, just occasionally, the seemingly impossible can happen. If her designer, Nigel Gresley could see her now, he'd be delighted.

Chapter Two
Genesis

I n 1919 Doncaster was a typical northern industrial town. Huge chimneys dotted the skyline, belching out thick, soot-laden smoke; hooters summoned workers to their factories, and everywhere was the smell of burning coal. It was a scene that had changed little for fifty years, and at the centre of the town was the locomotive, carriage and wagon works of the Great Northern Railway.

It was manufacturing on a gigantic scale. Steam hammers whistled upwards, paused for a second, and thundered down on to white-hot billets of steel in a crash and a shower of sparks. Expert craftsmen toiled over metal and wood, turning raw, unwilling materials into the precision-made components that, once assembled into their final form, delivered goods and carried passengers over a region ranging from London through Hertfordshire and into the flat countryside of Cambridgeshire, Nottinghamshire, Lincolnshire and Yorkshire. The noise had to be heard to be believed, and above all this din rang the riveting of the boilermakers, their work vital in assembling the boilers of the Great Northern's steam locomotives. It was organised chaos, and, after years of wartime armaments production, Doncaster Works was turning its hand to its primary occupation.

It wasn't all noise, though. As with every big industrial site, there were odd oases of quiet, and in one of these, Nigel Gresley, the Chief Mechanical Engineer of the railway, was deep in thought. A vicar's son of Norman ancestry and from a privileged background, he was a giant of a man, comfortably over six feet tall, and strongly built. He was keen on sports, and by all accounts had boundless enthusiasm. His friends, ironically, called him 'Tiny'. Pictures of him are few, but show a man with thick, wavy hair and a moustache. His face was soft but not round, and he looked more than anything like a kindly uncle. Although, at 43, he was the youngest CME of a major railway in Britain, he had toiled long and hard to reach his position: For the moment, he was stumped by one challenge in particular.

In the eighteen months or so he had been in the job before the First World War, it had become apparent that the most powerful passenger locomotives in the Great Northern fleet, the 'Atlantics' designed by his predecessor Henry Ivatt, would soon be hard pressed to haul heavier and faster trains. During the war, loads had got heavier still, but, because speeds were restricted, the Atlantics were able to perform adequately. Now, with a return to pre-war schedules imminent, and with a new generation of passenger coaches on the horizon, the express passenger locomotives would need to be replaced sooner rather than later with something much faster and more powerful. The question was: 'with what?' There were no easy answers.

Gresley at least had the benefit of other people's experience to guide him, and by the end of the First World War, pretty much every problem that the steam railway could face had been met – and conquered – somewhere in the world. In Britain at the time most passenger locomotives had eight or ten wheels, plus a tender carrying coal and water which they hauled immediately behind the cab. At the front they typically had four wheels in a sub-frame called a bogie to guide them round curves, then four or six wheels coupled together and linked to gigantic pistons, and in some cases, a pair of small wheels underneath the cab to offer some support. In the 'Whyte notation' system, this meant that the locomotives were described as '4-4-2' – or Atlantics. Gresley wanted to go one step further, to a 4-6-2, or 'Pacific', which offered the possibility of a quantum leap in boiler size and power, but in Britain at least, nobody had yet built a successful 'Pacific'.

Although Gresley's choice of career may well have disappointed his parents, his love of engineering and passion for railways meant that he was always destined for a role on the iron road. What is more, his varied experience had given him the knowledge to filter out the best practice from other railways and to apply it to the Great Northern. He started his career as an apprentice with the London & North Western Railway – the biggest player in the West Coast alliance – at Crewe Works, one of the finest locomotive works in the world. This was in 1893, a time when the famous 'Races to the North' between companies operating the East Coast route from King's Cross and their West Coast competitors working out of Euston, had provided a spur for improved designs. Gresley made the most of this, and then by the turn of the century, he moved north to the Lancashire & Yorkshire Railway, which was building some extremely advanced locomotives for the time, where he worked in the drawing office at Horwich and then the test room and materials workshop. After that he moved to Blackpool, where he became running shed foreman and gained a practical understanding of day-to-day railway operation. He moved on to take over the carriage and wagon department at the Great Northern Railway's Doncaster works in 1905. This effectively made him the company's engineering number two – and his senior, Henry Ivatt, was due to retire by 1911.

Ivatt had transformed the GNR from a traditional Victorian railway into a mid-table premier-league player with some modern and extremely capable designs. Many express locomotives (except on the Great Western Railway, GWR) were 4-4-0s, but Ivatt added a pair of trailing wheels to make them 4-4-2s, which meant that the engine could be longer and the firebox area bigger, allowing the engines to create more steam. In the early years of the twentieth century, these 'Atlantics' were competent if hungry performers, able to keep schedules with the loads then common. But one of the reasons that by 1919 the GNR needed more powerful engines was that Gresley had designed and built a new generation of carriages that transformed the passenger experience, being much more airy than most in use on the Great Northern, smoother riding and running more freely.

In 1911 Gresley was just thirty-five years old, and his skill and good work as Ivatt's number two ensured his succession:

the youngest Chief Mechanical Engineer among his contemporaries by a considerable margin. For the new CME of a railway company, the temptation is always to produce the fastest, most glamorous engines possible – the express passenger locomotives. In today's road-dominated society, though, it's very difficult to realise how totally dominant the railways were for transporting goods a century ago. For the Great Northern Railway, that meant it had to move coal from Yorkshire, fish from Grimsby, bricks from Peterborough, produce from Lincolnshire, and everything and anything else that anyone in its territory wanted moving.

Gresley's first locomotives therefore had to be goods engines, and he simply built further batches of Ivatt's designs: why reinvent the wheel for the sake of it? The first of Gresley's own designs were of the 2-6-0, or 'Mogul' type. They were designed to perform on a range of duties, from slow goods trains to fast passenger turns, and proved highly successful, though successive evolutions of his first 'Mogul' never cured a reputation for rough riding. Gresley had planned to build a new generation of express locomotives in 1915, but the First World War forced non-essential construction to be postponed, and Doncaster Works was turned over to the war effort. (Gresley himself was a member of the engineering committee of the Ministry of Food – and was awarded a CBE for his efforts in 1920.)

Initial plans were for something with a bigger boiler than Ivatt's Atlantics, and an extra pair of driving wheels. The 4-6-2 (or 'Pacific') arrangement gave fifty per cent more grip and allowed a much bigger boiler and firebox to be carried.

The problem was that building cylinders outside the wheels able to cope with that much steam presented a problem: they would obliterate platform edges from King's Cross to York, and that most definitely wouldn't do. The solution was simply to use the space between the frames to hold more cylinders. There was nothing new in this; most locomotives on the Great Northern had their two cylinders between the frames, and other railways were starting to use four cylinders to cope with the output offered by bigger boilers.

This seemed the way forward, so Gresley used the lull in building caused by the war to fit a Large Atlantic with four cylinders to see the effect. Results were inconclusive. The locomotive certainly accelerated well, but once up to speed, the boiler couldn't feed the four cylinders fast enough to make them worthwhile; sometimes the engine literally ran out of puff. This led Gresley to the far-reaching decision not to use four cylinders in future designs. But if four cylinders weren't the answer, what was? There was no way that the board of directors would countenance making clearances big enough for the huge outside cylinders needed for a larger boiler with just two of them, which left only one option: to go for three. At the time the use of three cylinders was not unknown in Britain, but it was far from the norm. Theoretically it offered the ability to use all the steam a big boiler could generate, with an extra bonus that, like the Manxman's mythical three-pedalled bicycle, it would offer extremely smooth delivery of power.

Gresley began by experimenting with a three-cylinder version of his heavy freight locomotives, which proved highly successful. A first was the use of 'conjugated valve gear': an arrangement almost unique to Gresley by which the actions of the valves in the two cylinders outside the wheels move the valves on the middle cylinder between the wheels. This makes maintenance easier under good conditions and gives more space between the wheels to deal with the piston from the cylinder. But, if Gresley's vision of a new generation of express locomotives was going to work, the valve gear would have to work at high speeds. And this needed to be proved quickly, because by 1919 Ivatt's Large Atlantics were really struggling with the loadings post-war conditions demanded of them. Before he was prepared to build his big new design, though, he wanted to confirm that his plans for new larger boilers would work in practice.

Gresley's ambitions for big three-cylinder locomotives depended on teaming a free-steaming boiler with a chassis similar to that of his latest freight locomotives. So he built another type of 'Mogul' which combined the two. The K3, with the widest boiler then fitted to a British locomotive, proved successful, but could the principles it embodied be used on an express locomotive? By 1922, Gresley was ready to put his ideas to the test. At that time, British experience with 'Pacifics' was limited to one unsuccessful prototype built by the Great Western Railway. Could he, and the Great Northern, really afford to take such a gigantic risk? Gresley looked overseas to see the latest American developments.

Back in 1911 the American Locomotive Company (ALCO) had built a prototype express locomotive for possible sale to railways across the United States and Canada, and very quickly the Pennsylvania Railroad based its K4 design on it. The K4 was a 'Pacific', but more crucially, the boiler was designed for very high outputs at high speeds; it was designed to cruise at 60mph, and in the event, proved comfortable cruising at 80mph. In 1916 *Engineer* had published a series of comprehensive analyses of the K4 and its performance, and, though he never admitted it, it is almost inconceivable that Gresley read the articles and didn't recognise immediately that a K4, or something like it, would be perfect for the Great Northern. Of course, the K4, like most American designs, was *way* too big to fit under bridges and alongside platforms in Britain. But that didn't matter: the proportions were right, and those *could* be adapted to fit the British structure gauge.

All the elements Gresley had spent the past few years working towards were now in place, and Doncaster Works was ready, willing and able to deliver something spectacular. After all, it would be the Great Northern's swan-song, and they wanted to ensure that the venerable old lady went out in a blaze of glory.

The reason it was the swan-song for the Great Northern, and just about every other railway company in Britain, was an impending restructuring of the industry. The railways were utterly exhausted after the First World War. They had performed prodigiously, moving everything needed to sustain a four-year struggle, and, not unnaturally, maintenance of locomotives, coaches, wagons and track had suffered. They needed time and money to catch up, but they were given neither. The government, impressed with the way the railways had operated under state control during the war, wanted to rationalise the huge number of railway companies, preferably into one. It had a clear choice – nationalise, or leave market forces to exert their will. So, after lengthy deliberations which initially envisaged a hybrid of seven regional companies in 1919, it was finally decided to merge almost all of Britain's railways into four (now known as 'The Grouping') from 1923, with a proviso that nationalisation could, possibly, take place twenty-five years later.

All of this was in the future, albeit the imminent future, when in April 1922 Doncaster Works released a giant of an express engine, the first fruit of Gresley's experiments. She bore the number 1470 and above her giant driving wheels wore the proud name *Great Northern*. To the average punter she must have seemed like she'd arrived from a different planet. She was enormous, and clearly based on the proportions of the K4, despite anything Gresley might say later. After initial tests she went into service between Doncaster and London and performed with flying colours. The new class of locomotive was known as A1, and never has such a suitable name been given to a design. Gresley had finally entered locomotive designer superstardom.

Later that year, *Great Northern* acquired a sister, No. 1471 *Sir Frederick Banbury*, named after a director of the Great Northern implacably opposed to the Grouping that was to come. In the run-up to the Grouping, in September 1922, she hauled a special train between London and Grantham weighing 100 tonnes more than the heaviest allowed on the GNR – to the fastest time allowed for the Flying Scotsman train (known officially as 'The Special Scotch Express'). It was a powerful statement of intent and capability, and the purse strings of the GNR's board of directors were loosened for the final time: they ordered a production batch of ten A1s. The first wouldn't be delivered until after the Grouping, and she wouldn't even be named, but even before the first metal was cut, she was given the number 1472. She would build on the experience gained on the first two Pacifics. The world didn't know it, but in the heart of Yorkshire, the finest artistry Doncaster has ever produced was taking shape in the Great Northern's works: an icon that within just five years would become a legend.

Chapter Three
The Great Show

I n January 1923 the planned Grouping of Britain's railway companies into four regional giants finally happened. In a year full of momentous events, this was one of the most significant and far-reaching in Britain. This was the year Howard Carter discovered the tomb of Tutankhamen, the year the BBC received its licence to broadcast, and for those rich enough to afford a radio, the year when they could buy a copy of the *Radio Times* at the princely cost of tuppence. It was a long, long time ago.

The Irish civil war was still raging (though it would end in April), and the airlines made their first faltering lurches into the skies, carrying rich and daring passengers in what were converted First World War bombers that struggled to reach 100mph. For most, however, the prospect of flying – or indeed driving a car – was unthinkably distant: the overwhelming majority of Britons were far too poor to even dream of such things.

With all this happening, it's small wonder that when the first production A1, No. 1472, emerged from Doncaster Works on 24 February, the world didn't sit up and take notice. Yet this was a hugely significant day: the first of Gresley's flagship design in series production – the first new express locomotive of the newly formed London & North Eastern Railway (LNER). No. 1472 cost £7,944: a trifle today, but a serious investment back then when £1,000 a year was a massive wage that only those near the top of the corporate ladder could dream of. As the first of the new Pacifics to be delivered after Grouping, she was presented to the LNER's directors in a private ceremony at Marylebone station.

The LNER, into which the Great Northern was now sub-sumed, was a colossus whose arms stretched from London throughout East Anglia, up to Newcastle and Edinburgh, the very farthest tip of Scotland, and even across the Pennines to Manchester: it was, by any measure, a massive undertaking, exceeded in size only marginally by its west-coast-line rival, the London, Midland & Scottish Railway (LMS).

One of this giant's biggest headaches was to decide who should be its Chief Mechanical Engineer. This person would have the enviable task of controlling engineering matters from Stratford in London to the Moray Firth, and the destinies of 7,400 locomotives. This appointment was not a simple matter, because Gresley faced two other extremely capable candidates. The most senior was John Robinson, the CME of the Great Central, who had provided it with a wide range of really good locomotives, and had proved far from afraid to innovate. His heavy freight design, in particular, was as close as the railways got at that time to a national standard. The other candidate was Sir Vincent Raven of the North Eastern Railway. Raven had also proved he could walk the walk as well as talking the talk and, at almost the same time as the Great Northern introduced the A1s, had launched his own design of Pacific, No. 2400.

From the start, the LNER was an unequal partnership. The North Eastern Railway was the biggest and most powerful single company within the group; and, with its electrification, air-brakes, and signalling systems, it was the most advanced too. If Robinson had seniority, then Raven could certainly have argued that, in technological terms, the North Eastern's culture of innovation and long-term planning should earn him the job.

Robinson probably tilted the tables in Gresley's favour by withdrawing from the contest on the grounds of age, and recommending the GNR's young CME as the best choice. Even so, it can't have been an easy call for the LNER directors. They picked Gresley, gambling on his potential rather than on what he had delivered to date – but they unquestionably got the decision absolutely right. Raven was said to have been so disgusted by the decision that he emigrated. His son-in-law, an austere but not unkindly looking man called Edward Thompson, worked with Raven at the North Eastern, and he too was bitterly disappointed that Gresley got the job. Thompson was an able designer who would have risen through the ranks in most companies. He became carriage and wagon superintendent after a couple of years heading the North Eastern's York carriage works, and the sublime coaches of the 1920s and 1930s are testament to his skill. Even so, he would never find himself quite able to accept Gresley's appointment, and would, eventually, wreak a horrible revenge (as described in Chapter 6).

While there was much reorganisation to do, one of the most crucial tasks for the engineering teams was to decide which of the two new express locomotive designs should be continued – Gresley's A1, or Raven's equivalent. In June 1923 a series of comparative trials between Gresley's 1472 and Raven's 2400 took place. By and large, performance was adequate for both – but, crucially, Gresley's design offered a 10 per cent saving in coal consumption, and was far better designed from a maintenance point of view, thanks to the conjugated valve gear.

Clearly, Gresley might naturally favour his own designs, but this shows his open-mindedness in being willing to evaluate his options. In truth, it was always likely that Gresley's design would win. It was based on rational development, whereas Raven, possibly out of a sense of rivalry with his younger counterpart, simply expanded one of his existing designs, when a fresh approach might have worked better. Still, there's no denying that Raven's Pacifics were elegant machines that were able to fulfil their duties for the next decade or so.

At this point, the history books might have been expected to show an uneventful process of rational evolution of Gresley's designs without the passengers the locomotives hauled noticing. History, though, as so often happens, was to throw a peculiar spanner in the works, thanks to that wonderfully British desire to try and make light of difficult circumstances.

The Empire Exhibition of 1924 was a classically British response to the problem that, having won the greatest of all wars up to that time, the country was now suffering a crisis of confidence. The British Empire, one must remember, was very much the *British Empire* at the time, and demanded respect. So a vast exhibition showing off the glories of the biggest empire the world has ever seen was planned for West London at Wembley. The British were going to have fun, and they were jolly well going to have it in style. In 1924 this was perhaps the most spectacular place on the planet. It really was. In the National Railway Museum in York there are pictures of matelots – yes, matelots! – rowing ecstatic sightseers down an artificial lake created especially for the event. It must have been utterly dazzling. And of course, as the country which invented the railways, perhaps the greatest contribution of the English-speaking world to date, it would be remiss not to showcase the latest developments.

To that end, the organisers scoured the railways of Britain for the latest developments. Above all, two stood out. The first was Gresley's new Pacific locomotive, the biggest passenger locomotive in Britain, and one of the most elegant pieces of engineering sculpture there has ever been. The second was the Great Western's latest locomotive, the smaller, but equally perfectly formed *Caerphilly Castle*. They were, and are, gorgeous.

The Great Western had the name for their exhibit decided, but for the nascent LNER, the question was which locomotive to send, and what to do with it. In 1923 the company had finally made official what for something like fifty years had been unofficial: the 10.00 departure from King's Cross to Edinburgh was named 'The Flying

Scotsman'. The question was whether the LNER could afford to take one of their latest engines out of service. Their dilemma was solved when No. 1472, the third engine in the fleet, failed severely. She faced the prospect of being out of action for some time, and was thus an ideal candidate to send to Wembley without affecting the service any more than her enforced absence already had. Then somebody within the LNER came up with a stroke of genius. The company wanted to promote itself to the public, and its most famous train was 'The Flying Scotsman'. 'The Flying Scotsman', being a train that could be formed of any locomotive and coaches if need be, clearly couldn't be there – but what if they named No. 1472 *after the train?* At a stroke, the LNER transformed the Flying Scotsman from a column in the timetable into living metal. That metal would promote the company, promote the train and, crucially, provide an evocative, resounding name that would put the Great Western's in the shade. From this point on, No. 1472 ceased to be a regular locomotive: she became a legend. However, it's not entirely clear where the name came from. It's known that in the nineteenth century the train that bore the official title of the 'Special Scotch Express' was very quickly nick-named the 'Flying Scotsman', and this most likely referred to its relative speed – though the temptation for wags bidding goodbye to Scots heading north from London to call it the 'Fleeing Scotsman' must have been irresistible! Either way, the Special Scotch Express was renamed, and No. 4472 (as she was renumbered at the end of 1923) was given appropriate nameplates.

She was repainted at Doncaster in a high-gloss, varnished beautiful apple green which Gresley despised. He ordered that it should be 'flatted down', but, happily, for once his orders seem to have been ignored. Packed in a special wrapping, she was sent to Wembley in her full glory. She was ready to take the plaudits her builders felt she deserved. They weren't disappointed by *Flying Scotsman*'s reception: she looked spectacular, and, though she remained static, she was fitted with a hidden electric motor driving her huge wheels and motion. She was one of the exhibition's star attractions. How many boys, on seeing this sparkling apple-green colossus, decided there and then that they wanted to be engine drivers? It must have been thousands – among them, a four-year-old boy from a wealthy family in Retford called Alan Pegler.

If the LNER was pleased with the public acclaim given to *Flying Scotsman*, it was far less happy with a display next to her: the Great Western boldly claimed that the smaller *Caerphilly Castle* was the most powerful express passenger locomotive in the world. Surely, the visitors must have wondered, *Caerphilly Castle* couldn't be more powerful than *Flying Scotsman* – could she? The Great Western argued that with a tractive effort (a theoretical measure to work out how much weight an engine could pull) of 31,500lbs, compared with *Flying Scotsman*'s 29,835lbs, it was clear: the Castle Class was the most powerful express passenger locomotive there was. On a pound-for-pound basis, the Great Western was ahead.

For the LNER, it must have seemed like somebody

arguing that their Mini could pull a caravan better than a Land Rover. With its bigger boiler, they argued, *Flying Scotsman* could keep pulling heavy loads at high speeds long after the Castles had run out of steam. That, they said, was the true measure of power. So it must have surprised them when the Great Western was prepared to rise to the challenge and agreed to test the Castle head-to-head against Gresley's flagship design.

With more A1s coming on stream, the LNER had enough in traffic in 1925 to agree to a series of trials with a Castle on its lines; in return, an A1 would go to the Great Western to see how Gresley's design performed on a different route. There is no definitive answer as to which side originated the trial. It has been suggested that the Great Western offered the trial as a kind of bet, knowing that Gresley, with his fiercely competitive nature, would be unable to resist. But it's also entirely possible that Gresley requested the trial himself in a spirit of honest engineering inquiry: if the Great Western's claims for the Castle Class were true, there might be something to learn from it. We have already seen Gresley's willingness to learn from others' experience, so it seems likely that the request to compare a Castle with an A1 was about engineering rather than point-scoring.

In April 1925 the Great Western sent No. 4079 *Pendennis Castle* to King's Cross shed for the first series of trials on the East Coast Main Line. She was seemingly diminutive alongside the A1s at King's Cross, and onlookers must have confidently expected her to struggle with the 456-tonne load as she climbed out of the station and on the greasy rails through Gasworks Tunnel on her way north. The air of anticipation, particularly among the senior management of the LNER, must have been almost tangible. Finally, the Great Western's claims of power would be shown up in the most public manner.

If they were unnerved by the doubtless partisan support for the LNER, *Pendennis Castle*'s driver and fireman didn't show it. Simmering at the safety valves, the Great Western locomotive awaited the guard's whistle and at its shrill blast eased her way through the tracery of pointwork outside the station without any sign of struggle or slipping: something the A1s found difficult. Time and time again, *Pendennis Castle* got to grips with her heavy loads and up to speed in times that staggered even King's Cross's most ardent speed merchants. Passing times of 5 minutes 30 seconds at Finsbury Park with 330 tonnes were beyond reach of the A1s tested in comparison. The LNER's driver was criticised for not rising to the challenge – 'unenterprising' is the word used in every account of the trials – but it's unlikely this made much difference. On the LNER's home turf Gresley's A1s had been found sorely wanting.

Later that year, though, the LNER sent an A1, No. 4474 *Victor Wild*, to Swindon for trials on the Great Western, and here a very different picture emerged. Given instructions to drive to the timetable, Driver Pibworth and his fireman swiftly got used to the Welsh coal the Great Western burned, and proved that the A1s were easily able to match the stiffest times set for the Castles. Better still, among the steep hills of Devon, where even the Castles struggled, the huge reserves of power provided by the A1's big boiler allowed her to race over them at speeds the Great Western was quite unable to match with the same loads. Ultimately therefore, the trials resulted in an honourable draw, with both designs acquitting themselves well, although the Castle's coal consumption was substantially lower than Gresley's design.

Pendennis Castle's performance at King's Cross still rankled with the critics, though. 'Aha,' they exclaimed, 'it's the Castle's higher boiler pressure that made the difference. The LNER must match it to get the best results.' Gresley wasn't convinced, and with good reason.

It's true that the Castle's boiler pressure of 225psi made a difference against the A1's 180psi, but there were other, more subtle factors at play that explained why *Pendennis Castle* was able to start so smoothly from King's Cross and get up to speed so quickly. The first is a simple one: the Castle had no trailing wheels, and that meant that, when the back end of the locomotive dipped as the weight of the train pulled on it at starting, all the weight was on the driving wheels, giving her more grip. When an A1 started, her back end also dipped, but, because she had a pair of small trailing wheels supporting the cab and firebox, some of the weight shifted from her six driving wheels, giving her slightly less grip when starting. With a heavy load, that can make all the difference.

Even more subtle, but ultimately of far more importance than boiler pressure and weight transfer, was the fact that, thanks to the Great Western's lengthy experiments with valves, the Castle's cylinders and pistons allowed her to make the best use of every ounce of steam. Gresley's valves were based on more orthodox practice, and were significantly less efficient. Steam was leaving the cylinders when it still had energy that could be used; quite simply, the Great Western was getting each pound of steam to do more work than the LNER was.

Gresley didn't want to change the A1s' design – why would he when they were doing great work already? – but he was open-minded enough to try some experiments. First, he altered the valves on his preferred guinea pig, No. 4477 *Gay Crusader*, to see what effect that would have. Satisfied with the results, he fitted boilers with a pressure of 225psi to a pair of locomotives, Nos. 2544 *Lemberg*, and 2580 *Enterprise* to see what the results of that were. Performance was somewhat better, although not enough so to justify the expense of altering the whole fleet. But what made the real difference was that the combined effect of the modifications showed a big reduction in the amount of coal burned, and for the perennially cash-strapped LNER that was important enough to induce Gresley to adopt GWR-style valves and higher boiler pressure. The resulting tweaked Pacifics were called A3s, and eventually, all the A1s would be converted to A3 specification. Though nobody knew it at the time, the stage was set for a period universally known as a golden age.

Chapter Four
The Golden Age

The period from around 1925 to the start of the Second World War was to be a high-water mark which, the critics say, has never been matched. It was a time – if you believe the publicity – when every train ran on time and was spotlessly clean, and when every passenger was served good solid food by white-suited waiters. Britain's railways really showed their mettle during this period, led by Gresley, *Flying Scotsman*, and the LNER. The country depended almost totally on the railways, to a degree unknown today. Every station had a goods shed where wagons could be loaded and unloaded, and a dizzying volume of freight trains ran here, there and everywhere. The national newspaper you bought in the morning would have been delivered by the railway overnight. The fish you bought in the Midlands had been carried from the ports by the railways, like coal from the mines, food from the farms, the mail: almost everything which had to be carried more than a few miles was sent by rail.

And that was just goods. The privileged few could, in theory, have driven long distances, but they didn't, because the railway was faster and the roads poor. If you wanted to travel in Britain in the 1920s and 1930s, the chances were that you went by train: there simply wasn't another option. Most people didn't need, and couldn't afford, to travel far.

It didn't stop the railways encouraging them to, though. As the A1s came on stream, the LNER really got to grips with its publicity and marketing. Time and time again, the company produced promotional materials of an elegance and sophistication that take the breath away even now. This was, in part, thanks to a recognition that of all the companies created by the Grouping, the LNER was by far the most fragile of the Big Four. In the absence of substance, the company would have to try to create style. While the other railways were either finding their feet or continuing pre-war-style marketing, the LNER really tapped into the *zeitgeist*. This was the 1920s, remember, and the growing art-deco school was something that, inadvertently, Gresley had anticipated with his smooth and clean design for the A1s. The time was right for a marketing genius to exploit the romance of the rails. And the LNER got lucky: it had two.

The first was William Teasdale, the former advertising manager of the North Eastern Railway. While many railways promoted themselves with fussy, stilted Edwardian elegance, Teasdale was different. He knew that if he could make the LNER appear glamorous, there was a good chance that the commuter crammed into his coaches on the way to London might just book holidays through the LNER rather than one of its competitors. Teasdale was extremely effective, separating the advertising department from what would now be called public relations and centralising promotion and marketing over the whole company.

Throughout the LNER's existence, it operated on a highly decentralised basis, and only a handful of functions were applied across the whole company. Marketing was one of them, and it was brilliant.

Teasdale's approach went for simplicity. Rather than trying to extol every possible virtue of a resort or a service, he chose to focus on one specific aspect. A typical example was his decision to continue using the famous 'Jolly Fisherman' poster that the Great Northern Railway had used to promote Skegness. It was a bright image combined with a simple message, and it worked. High-profile artists were commissioned to paint posters, and very quickly the LNER's glamorous image was assured.

Teasdale's decision to have a separate press office also paid dividends, and the LNER soon proved highly adept at manipulating the media to project the image of a fast, progressive railway. Teasdale left and was replaced by Cecil Dandridge in 1927. Dandridge made few alterations to the LNER's marketing strategy, and he continued the tradition of holding open days at locations around the system. These open days were a great way of showing off the company's latest developments to areas that hadn't, and perhaps never would, get any benefit from them. They offered footplate rides, demonstrations of signalling and the latest technology, the newest coaches, and of course, the very latest locomotives were present. The public was often charged for admission, but this was offset by the fact that the proceeds went to charity, often a benevolent fund for railwaymen. They were incredibly popular, particularly with children, but also with adults – and even today, though there is perhaps one such event in Britain every couple of years, open days and exhibitions remain very well-attended.

But while the marketing was top-notch, it masked a horrifying underlying problem: the LNER was broke. The East Coast Main Line was probably profitable, as were the lucrative Yorkshire coalfields, but the myriad lines serving the farthest reaches of the Fens, of Lincolnshire, the high moors of Yorkshire and the Highlands of Scotland must have been marginal at best. Even Gresley's genius couldn't find a way to build the new modern locomotives the company so desperately needed for its bread-and-butter business for nothing.

That didn't stop him and his team continuing to innovate, however. The power of the A1s meant that for the first time, a railway company had a locomotive able to run over really long distances with a reasonable load. This in turn had the potential to open up new commercial opportunities and generate operational efficiencies too. The A1s could haul enough coal in the tender and scoop up water at a series of troughs laid between the rails en route, to get themselves 400-or-so miles without problems. The limitation was human: to ask a driver – and, more particularly, a fireman – to work at full capacity without a break for up to seven hours was beyond even the working practices of the day. In fact, if done on a regular basis, it would have been downright dangerous. The question must have reverberated in Gresley's head: 'How can I change the engine crews without stopping the train?' The obvious answer was to slow the train down to walking pace, let the new crew jump on, and the old one off, but this was clearly a non-starter: it would be dangerous, unreliable and, if the train was moving at walking pace, pointless. Asking driver and fireman to climb over the top of the tender was equally ridiculous. In the absence of a teleporter, Gresley was stumped.

Then he had a brainwave. For years passengers had been travelling from one coach to another by corridors at the end of them. It was well established (the Great Northern had been one of the pioneers), so what would stop the engineers putting a corridor in the tender so that the crew could pass from the coach to the engine's cab? Providing he kept the dimensions of the corridor fairly small, he wouldn't sacrifice that much coal or water capacity, and he could always make the tender longer to compensate if needed.

To test his theory, he arranged an experiment in his own dining room. He laid out his chairs in the pattern he had in mind for the tender and then tried to crawl through the space; he reasoned that if a relative giant of a man like himself could get through, so could most of his crews. As he was crawling through this impromptu maze, one of his daughters walked in — one can imagine the looks that must have passed between doting father and a thoroughly confused daughter, who presumably went scurrying from the room to fetch the men in white coats. Thankfully, they were delayed, because Gresley's 'eureka' moment was a cracker, and he was allowed to perpetuate it in metal.

Secret orders were sent to the LNER's main works at Doncaster to build a tender with a corridor in it. On no account must word slip out, because Dandridge and his marketing team had come up with a plan that would guarantee headlines for days – the longest non-stop rail journey in the world – and it depended on the corridor tender. The commercial justification for this was flimsy at best, but the LNER's board was shrewd enough to know that the publicity from such a record-breaking, epoch-making run would have what would nowadays be known as a 'halo effect' on all of the LNER's other passenger services, whether justified or not. It was worth taking the risk. The LNER was going to run a train non-stop from King's Cross in London to the Scottish citadel of Edinburgh's Waverley station: a distance of 392 miles.

In Cold War-style secrecy, the tender was built, and to test it, placed behind an old Ivatt Atlantic. The driver was guaranteed a clear road north to Doncaster on a test train (ostensibly for braking trials) but found himself stopped at Retford. He called the signalman in a fury.

'I've got a clear road,' he must have said, probably in the colourful invective often used by drivers in such circumstances. 'What's going on?'

'Oh, you've got a clear road,' the signalman said. 'I stopped you because I wanted to see this new corridor tender.'

Gresley would have fallen off his chair, had he heard the conversation, but the railway grapevine is both notoriously leaky within, and deadly silent without when it matters. So it proved this time. Gresley's corridor tender was too good a secret to keep from the LNER, but the staff knew how high the stakes were and ensured that this open secret was an open secret only within the LNER. The game was on.

There were, though, a couple of minor problems with *Flying Scotsman* that would prevent it getting much farther north than Newcastle. The most critical was that, even though *Flying Scotsman* was a shrunk-down version of an American design, she was still too tall for some of the bridges on the former North British route from Newcastle to Edinburgh, and the platform edges at Newcastle Central station were awfully close to being hit by the A1s, even at low speed. This didn't deter Gresley. He decided to cut down the height of the locomotive's chimney, boiler dome and cab to ensure she wouldn't knock any bits off. Doing this had no effect on performance but it did have a big effect on her appearance. With the cab roof now almost flush, she looked sleeker and more purposeful, as if, like a racehorse, she'd got her nose down in preparation for some fast running. To save potential embarrassment at Newcastle, a small section of plate just below the buffers was cut away, and no more was heard from the civil engineers about it.

Thanks to LNER's crack marketing team, the press was made discreetly aware of the run, and *Flying Scotsman* was specially transferred from Doncaster to King's Cross to head the first departure. The date set was 1 May 1928, May Day, and on an otherwise unassuming Tuesday, King's Cross was thronged with dignitaries, reporters, well-wishers, enthusiasts, passengers and railwaymen eager to see history made.

Flying Scotsman's driver that day was Albert Pibworth, the same man who had shown such mettle during the locomotive exchanges on the Great Western. At 11.00 that morning, *Flying Scotsman* sallied forth on her way north and into the history books. Never before had anything like this been attempted, yet here was the LNER not only going for it, but on a regular basis, and in both directions, for at the same time, an identical train hauled by No. 2580 *Shotover* eased its way east out of Edinburgh Waverley on a non-stop run to London.

Flying Scotsman's journey was scheduled to take 8 hours 15 minutes, which – because of agreements between the rival East and West Coast alliances of pre-grouping days following the races to the north – was the same as the stopping time, and at Tollerton, just north of York, Pibworth was relieved by his Gateshead counterpart Tommy Blades for the final run to Edinburgh. Crowds thronged the lineside, and as *Flying Scotsman* got closer to Edinburgh, it was clear that she still had plenty in hand. Without even trying, Blades managed to get *Flying Scotsman* and her train into Waverley station 12 minutes early. The plaudits were showered on *Flying Scotsman* and her designer – whatever the future was to hold, both were now certain of their place in the history books.

The non-stop run is crucial, not just in the story of *Flying Scotsman* and Nigel Gresley, but in the development of passenger trains too. Until then, nobody had even thought to try running such long distances non-stop: by today's standards, even most express trains were horribly slow, and, while *Flying Scotsman*'s non-stop run was in one sense pointless, as it was no faster than the usual service with stops at major stations, it pointed the way forward powerfully. It was clear that the timings between London and Scotland were artificially slow, thanks to the new generation of rolling stock being introduced.

The *Flying Scotsman* ran non-stop between London and Edinburgh for the summer of 1928, reverting to its usual pattern in the winter timetable. The following year, in the summer, the non-stop service restarted with a blitz of publicity. The A1s and their more powerful counterparts the A3s were dominating East Coast Main Line services, and though the Great Western continued to claim dominance in the power stakes, thanks to an enlarged design of Castle known as the 'Kings', in truth, there was nothing on the rails in Britain which could match the performance of Gresley's thoroughbreds on a daily basis. Gresley and his team were approaching the pinnacle of their genius.

It's a sign of the fame of *Flying Scotsman* and her namesake train that in 1929 one of the first talking films produced in Britain was called *The Flying Scotsman* and had her as the second leading lady. (Gresley, it's fair to say, seems unlikely to have been consulted about it, and if he had, it's unlikely that the producers would ever have been given the go-ahead.) The plot is a conventional one of love and mis-understanding, and the crucial moment involves the heroine, played by Pauline Johnson, pulling a point lever to divert the carriages from crashing into the engine, saving her heart-throb from disaster. These days, it's unintentionally hilarious – as the clips in the National Railway Museum show – but at the time it must have seemed quite realistic.

Gresley, though, was furious, concerned that people might actually believe the LNER's safety systems were as flimsy as those in the film. After hurried negotiations, the film-makers put in a disclaimer warning that artistic licence had been taken, and that the safety procedures shown were definitely not those of the LNER!

A couple of years later, *Flying Scotsman* received a high-profile visitor at her King's Cross base. An Indian prince – His Highness Pratap Singh, Maharaja of Nabha, no less – was invited by the LNER's press office to pay a visit. *Flying Scotsman* had been specially prepared for her visitor, and under close guidance the prince took the controls. At 10mph, she covered 100 yards before the brakes were applied and the Prince's trip of a lifetime ended. It's a sign of how famous *Flying Scotsman* was that the LNER chose to invite the young prince to see her rather than any of the more powerful A3s.

By 1929 the Great Western was sitting back in terms of locomotive innovation, content in the knowledge that its fleet would do all the work needed of it for a generation to come, and that only replacements for worn-out and life-expired rolling stock were needed. The Southern Railway was beginning an extensive electrification programme, and, by and large, its steam developments were seen as stop-gaps; and the London, Midland & Scottish Railway was only just beginning to find its feet after a tumultuous period of reorganisation. Only Gresley and the LNER had any mind to continue developing the steam locomotive, though one could argue convincingly that, such was the performance of the A1s and A3s, all that was needed was a freight locomotive using the same boiler and a really useful mixed-traffic design along the lines of the Great Western's Hall class.

Gresley had other ideas and wanted to explore the possibilities of using marine-type boilers on a steam loco-motive. On many ships, boilers worked at a much higher pressure and then used the exhaust steam from one high-pressure cylinder to drive larger but lower-pressure cylinders in a process known as compounding. They were much more efficient than the simple-expansion process used in most steam locomotives, but also more complicated. There had been some successful compound designs in Britain, but most had been found wanting. Gresley thought he could make it work in a large express locomotive, and in great secrecy he prepared designs for a radical new engine to be built at Darlington. In December 1929, he introduced, with great fanfare, No. 10000. This streamlined giant of a locomotive – bigger than *Flying Scotsman* – was painted battleship grey and looked like nothing else on the rails before or since. Gresley's aim had been to reduce coal consumption, but, although No. 10000 proved extremely powerful, she was also a hungry and unreliable performer. Only when she was rebuilt with a conventional boiler in the 1930s would she start to show how successful she could have been.

The 1929 Wall Street crash hit the LNER hard, decimating much of its traffic, and in a bid to keep costs down, jobs were cut and strict limits imposed on overtime. It wasn't unusual either for huge numbers of trains to be cancelled in order to save coal: funds really were that tight.

Yet ironically, with Gresley's powerful Pacific loco-motives, the LNER was able, potentially, to offer a more attractive long-distance passenger service than ever before. Eventually, patience with the artificially low London to Edinburgh time of 8 hours and 30 minutes ran out, and in May 1932 it was cut by 45 minutes. Speed was starting to become important again – and not just in Britain.

The problems of Germany in the 1920s and 1930s are well-documented: hyper-inflation, high unemployment and rampant fascism. It wasn't until the 1930s that the country started to get on its feet again, and the price it paid for that was Hitler. The nationalised railway, Deutsche Reichsbahn, was among the most innovative in the world, and the Germans were amongst the first adopters of electric trains in regular service. Spurred on by heavy government invest-ment, Deutsche Reichsbahn started developing high-speed trains using alternatives to steam. (One used an aero engine to drive a propeller; it reached fantastic speeds, but under-standably, railway bosses were concerned about the dangers of the propeller to bystanders.) Finally, though, the investment paid off, and in 1932 the Germans were able to announce that a new design of diesel train had hit 124mph on test – and that they hoped to introduce it into revenue-earning service the following year.

This design, which became known as 'The Flying Hamburger', offered a compelling and prophetic vision of the future of rail travel: it had no separate locomotive, relying instead on small but powerful diesel engines under the floor. These drove a generator to supply power to the electric motors which in turn drove the wheels; a new signalling system would apply brakes if the train exceeded the speed limit or passed a red signal. This articulated, two-car train was the weapon Deutsche Reichsbahn intended to use to fight the increasingly popular airlines on the crucial Berlin-to-Hamburg corridor. With a top speed of 100mph that it was easily able to reach in service, The Flying Hamburger was able to average 77mph consistently for the 178-mile journey. This was the future, and it had a massive impact.

Other countries too were experimenting with alternatives to steam. The French were introducing handsome, streamlined, petrol-driven railcars designed by the flamboyant automotive genius Ettore Bugatti, and in Britain the Great Western was contemplating introducing single-coach diesel trains to work on branch lines. Diesel trains offered a number of advantages over steam. They were cleaner and, because they didn't need smokeboxes emptying every day and water filling up throughout, were able to work longer between servicing. They were potentially faster and only needed one man on the footplate, rather than the driver and fireman that a steam locomotive required.

Most of the early diesel trains had just one or two coaches, but the LNER, always keen to save money, was sufficiently intrigued by the Flying Hamburger to send Gresley's assistant, Oliver Bulleid, over to Germany to take a look at it. Bulleid was impressed with the smoothness and speed of the German train, though he noted that it had suffered teething troubles. His report encouraged Gresley to take a look for himself, and Gresley immediately recognised that this train, or something like it, could revolutionise express passenger travel on the LNER. On his return, he asked the Germans to provide a detailed estimate for the LNER board of the impact of running a three-coach Flying Hamburger train between London and Newcastle, working to a four-hour schedule.

The Germans were scrupulously honest. The Flying Hamburger couldn't, they said, do better than four and a half hours between King's Cross and Newcastle. Even worse, because offering hot meals on the train would have been extremely difficult, due to space problems, the best that could be offered in terms of catering was a cold buffet service of the type popular in Germany. That, of course, wouldn't be nearly enough for diners more used to proper cooked meals with roast potatoes and Yorkshire puddings. It would have been a compromise too far for the LNER.

With further development, there is little doubt that a diesel train akin to the Flying Hamburger could have matched the LNER's needs, but already Gresley was thinking along different lines. While the question of catering seems to have struck the killer blow to aspirations to run high-speed diesel trains, Gresley reasoned that they were also expensive to buy and maintain, and in the 1930s their efficiency gains over steam were not that great. Furthermore, he knew that with a light load of something like 250 tonnes some types of steam locomotives were quite capable of very high average speeds. The free-steaming Castles of the Great Western were consistently averaging

75mph between Swindon and Paddington, while Gresley's own A1 and A3 Pacifics were also free-running and powerful.

Though there was some concern at board level about the state of the track in areas of extensive coal mining, Gresley was able to persuade the directors to allow some high-speed tests using an ordinary locomotive and carriages. It was planned to run with three coaches – a first-class corridor coach, a first-class and dining car and a kitchen car – and to this short rake would be added a dynamometer car: a coach fitted with sensitive measuring equipment that would be able to accurately record speed and location information. The load behind the locomotive would be something like 147 tonnes: a mere trifle. The plan was to run between King's Cross and Leeds in 2 hours 45 minutes each way: an average speed of 67.5mph.

To emphasise that standard equipment was being used, it was decided to use one of the early A1 Pacifics, rather than the uprated A3s. Of these, the LNER opted for No. 4472 *Flying Scotsman,* the company's flagship – though not, it must be said, the best of the fleet by any means. King's Cross driver William Sparshatt was chosen to drive the train because of his reputation as something of a speed merchant. Considerations of coal consumption simply didn't apply to him – he was definitely the right man for the job!

On 30 November 1934 *Flying Scotsman* charged out of King's Cross on her way north to Leeds. Sparshatt left observers in no doubt about the capabilities of *Flying Scotsman.* She charged the step gradient of Stoke Bank near

Grantham recording a minimum speed of 81mph, having already hit 94.75mph on the descent from Stevenage. Sparshatt arrived in Leeds thirteen minutes ahead of the schedule, in 151 minutes, and at an average speed of 73.4mph.

The northward run was so good that it was decided to add an extra couple of coaches for the return journey to London, taking the weight up to 207.5 tonnes. This time *Flying Scotsman* would have Stoke Bank, one of the greatest racing stretches of line anywhere in Britain, to hare down. First though, she had to climb five uphill miles at 1:200 from Grantham to reach the summit. Sparshatt had the bit between his teeth and thrashed *Flying Scotsman* uphill. Her chimney barked her exhaust note in blocks of furious defiance at this treatment, her fireman flung coal desperately into the firebox to keep the steam rate up, and finally she crested the summit of Stoke Bank at 68.5mph and got her nose down. The speed started rising on this magical stretch of line, and as it mounted, so did the air resistance at the front of the train, pushing like a giant hand trying to slow her down. She continued to accelerate towards the little station of Essendine, and just before she was compelled to slow down, the dynamometer car peaked at 100mph: the first time this had been verifiably recorded by a steam locomotive anywhere in the world. Undaunted, Sparshatt thrashed *Flying Scotsman* onward, racing her into King's Cross in a time of 157 minutes 17 seconds. It was a new record from Leeds to London and an amazing performance from driver, fireman and locomotive. It was starting to look as if

Gresley's belief that steam power could match the diesels might just be true.

The following year plans were put in hand for a test using one of the more powerful A3 Pacifics, No. 2750 *Papyrus*, this time to Newcastle. She averaged 68mph, recording a maximum of 88.5mph on the northbound run – proof that an A3 could run at high speeds for long periods. For the return, it was a slightly different story. This time, with Sparshatt again at the regulator, an official speed record attempt would be made on Stoke Bank. It surprised no one that between Doncaster and Grantham, Sparshatt nursed his charge, giving his fireman time to build up a really big, hot fire. *Papyrus* hit the summit of Stoke Bank at the same speed as *Flying Scotsman*, but from then on, the newer locomotive's better valves and higher boiler pressure started to tell. As she passed Little Bytham, eight miles downhill from the summit of Stoke Bank, she was averaging 96.9mph, and then went faster still on the 1:200 descent from there, hitting a record 108mph. She arrived in King's Cross in 231 minutes – well under the 4½ hours the Germans promised from The Flying Hamburger on the same route. *Papyrus* hadn't just beaten her sister's record: she'd smashed the unverified claims of competitors from Europe and America too. Gresley's Pacifics were the fastest steam locomotives in the world.

With the argument about whether steam could match newer technology well and truly sorted, Gresley turned his attention to designing a locomotive that could achieve the high averages of *Flying Scotsman* and *Papyrus* without over-working the fireman. He had built a new locomotive called

Cock o' the North, ostensibly for operation on the tough line between Edinburgh and Aberdeen. In truth, however, this machine was to be a guinea pig to test new ideas on. She had a wedge-shaped front and smoothed sides to reduce air resistance. She had a big boiler and a 2-8-2 wheel arrangement, so she had more grip than an A1 or A3. Gresley had high hopes and sent her over to the French test facility at Vitry to be evaluated scientifically. The news wasn't good, though: she was heavy on coal and her wheel bearings were prone to overheating.

For Gresley it was something of a disappointment, but he wasn't deterred – he decided instead to develop the A3, as *Papyrus* had shown that the fundamentals of the design were well able to cope with high speeds. What he had in mind was something akin to an A3 GT. Its fundamentals would be based on the older design, but improved: the boiler would be of 250psi instead of 220, the cylinders would have a different bore, and all the internal pipes that carried steam and water would be made as gently curved as possible to minimise resistance. The crowning glory would be an all-new streamlined casing similar in concept to that of No. 10000.

It took much experimentation in a wind tunnel to get the shape right, and it was with some trepidation that Gresley presented his proposals for a streamlined train to run between London and Newcastle, timed to coincide with the twenty-fifth anniversary of King George V's accession to the throne. It would be called, with prescient timing, the Silver Jubilee.

The board took its time considering Gresley's plans: it would cost a lot of money, but it might be worth it if the service proved a success. They gave the project the green light on the understanding that it would enter service on 30 September 1935. There was precious little time.

Four streamlined A3 GTs were to be built, given the classification A4. They would haul a new set of luxury coaches incorporating the latest developments, such as air-conditioning, an electric kitchen and separate restaurant cars for first and second class. In recognition of the Silver Jubilee theme, each locomotive's name would start with 'Silver', and both engine and coaches would be painted in a mixture of subtle greys.

The frames for the first locomotive, *Silver Link*, were laid on 26 June 1935, and less than a month later, she left Doncaster Works for trials. She was an absolute sensation. With her wedge-shaped streamlined front, she looked nothing like anything else on the rails, and her silver-grey colour scheme shone brilliantly amongst the apple-green of the other passenger locomotives.

Three days before the public launch, a demonstration trip for press and invited guests was held. Though LNER chairman Sir Ralph Wedgwood said no record attempt would be made, vases of cut flowers on the tables were removed by stewards before she set off. She was quickly up to speed and hared through Hitchin at 107mph. Soon afterwards Gresley himself was reluctantly forced to go through the corridor tender to tell the crew to slow down: 'Ease your arm young man,' he told driver Taylor. 'We have twice touched 112mph!' Taylor said he thought the train had only been travelling at around 90mph, so smooth was the ride, and Gresley softened: 'Go a bit easier, we have an old director in the back and he's getting a bit touchy.'

Gresley's A4 Pacific – the ultimate development of *Flying Scotsman* – was a massive success, and now that they had a locomotive able to run really fast, the LNER wasted little time in reaping the marketing benefits. Two more stream-lined trains were put into service: the 'Coronation', from London to Edinburgh, and the 'West Riding Limited', which ran from London to Leeds and Bradford. For *Flying Scotsman*, it marked the end of her career at the top of the locomotive league table. She was already outclassed by her close relations, the A3s, and the advent of the A4 meant *Flying Scotsman* was relegated to lesser duties, though always on the East Coast Main Line, and always on passenger trains.

Flying Scotsman, still in her original form, finally lost her corridor tender in October 1936 as more A4s came on stream. For eight years, she had been one of the flagship long-distance locomotives of the LNER, and though she wouldn't be asked to run such long distances non-stop, she remained a vital part of the front-line fleet at King's Cross. Life as a fleet engine was slightly different from the pampered-racehorse regime applied to the non-stop and streamlined trains. Those machines were given special attention at the engine sheds to ensure they were in tip-top condition: a failure on the 'Silver Jubilee' simply wouldn't do. It meant that *Flying Scotsman* and the other A1s received a very slightly lower standard of maintenance, in recognition that their duties weren't now as demanding as they once were.

The LNER's speed records were quickly beaten, first by the LMS and then by the Germans, who hit 124.5mph. Gresley wanted to see how fast his streamlined A4s could go, and on 3 July 1938, No. 4468 *Mallard* set an all-time record for steam of 126mph. The morale boost for the LNER, and indeed for Britain, was significant, but it made little difference to the day-to-day operation of the railways: the staff had enough on their plates with the day jobs.

It was the high-water mark for steam. Streamlined, advanced locomotives were hauling equally beautiful trains that exuded an air of glamour and style not seen since. Even if one had to travel daily on packed and filthy commuter trains, the sight of one of these trains passing by couldn't have failed to evoke an emotion similar to that of seeing *Concorde*. And the LNER had such panache: whether it was the streamlined A4s or the graceful and elegant A1s and A3s, its front-line locomotive fleet epitomised the art-deco ideals of cleanliness in design and pride in appearance. It may well have been a triumph of style over substance, but the LNER, and to a lesser extent the LMS and Great Western, have given us a compelling cultural memory of a gentler, more civilised and glamorous way of travelling. It truly was a golden era, and it was soon to come crashing down with the Second World War.

Chapter Five
Behind the Mask

I f our perception of the railways of the 1920s and 1930s is of a golden age, it's worth taking a moment to contrast this image with the everyday reality for those who had to keep the trains moving. Passengers on 'The Flying Scotsman' might have been able to relax in luxury, but the crew on the footplate had it anything but easy. It took drivers and firemen a long time to work their way up to their position – and that position was the steel footplate of a locomotive cab: dirty, hot, occasionally wet and draughty, and always extremely hard work.

Their careers started surprisingly early. The railways were seen as good employers, and in many areas competition for jobs was extremely stiff. Young boys (often fourteen in many companies, but seventeen in the LNER) who set their hearts on being engine drivers had a daunting path to follow. Firstly, they had to meet height and weight requirements. Then their grades at school had to be good, and only then would they stand a chance of being selected for an interview. And these interviews were demanding: there was such competition for places that the railways could choose the very best from the working classes. Coming from a railway family was often a big help, but even so far from a guarantee of success. If the lucky applicant passed the mental, physical and eyesight tests to the satisfaction of the railway, he would be taken on in the most menial job possible: engine cleaner.

On the face of it, cleaning engines sounds vastly removed from driving them, but the training process had been developed over many decades, and, with labour cheap, the railways were able to keep their precious locomotives clean despite all the coal and soot that inevitably covered them.

Being an engine cleaner was – and on today's heritage railways still is – a filthy job. Standards at many sheds were extremely high, and an army of eager young boys, armed with nothing more than a cotton rag and perhaps some brick dust, was tasked with cleaning their steeds. It's a job I've done on a heritage railway, and I can tell you that sitting on the top of a big boiler with no ropes or handholds and trying to clean a locomotive is not an easy task. It's very different from cleaning a car – not only is there a much bigger area to cover, there's very rarely a handhold where you want it, and everything seems set up either to give you a nasty whack whenever you move, or else to burn you, as the case may be. Then there are the rods and valve gear on the outside of the engine. These tarnish very easily, and get covered with thick, emulsified oil that's the very devil to banish. Locomotives had to leave their shed with shining rods, shining paintwork and no trace of the previous day's work: they were corporate flagships, and the old salts who ran the engine sheds made sure the cleaners knew it. In every sense, these young lads were at the very bottom of the heap.

But it wasn't all bad. Spending their time on and around

the locomotives, the cleaners got to know about them and how they worked. It was a gradual process of learning, and it worked well, gradually teaching these boys the complex and demanding rules and regulations of the railway, as well as the engineering behind the locomotives. Many studied extensively in their own time to learn as much as possible.

Only after a couple of years (it depended greatly on the company, and on the specific needs of the shed) was the young cleaner given more responsibility. Often this involved minding engines arriving on shed and carrying out further duties, such as ensuring that there was enough water in the boiler, or keeping a fire going. Gradually this increased until the lad had to pass an exam to move to the next level: that of fireman. He was on his way.

Steam locomotives relied on human input. Without care and attention the complex and heavy mechanisms that combined to move a train wouldn't perform to the high standard of reliability demanded by daily operations. Express locomotives often travelled hundreds of miles every day, and, on the long-distance East Coast Main Line trains from London to the north, a plentiful supply of steam from the boiler was always needed to keep the train moving and on time. It was the fireman's principal responsibility to manage a locomotive's energy levels by maintaining a healthy fire to produce the maximum amount of steam. In the case of *Flying Scotsman* the maximum boiler pressure was 180psi when she was built in 1923 as an A1 Pacific (she was later rebuilt as an A3 class), and the fireman had to maintain a pressure as close to the maximum as possible whilst at the same time not overstepping the mark, which would waste valuable steam.

Most new fireman would start out on shunting or lightly loaded pick-up goods trains. Then they moved up the ranks to take greater responsibility on local passenger and other similar duties. At the top of the chain were those who made it into the 'Top Link' – an elite group of firemen capable of managing the most demanding, challenging and important trains on the national railway network.

The role of the fireman has never changed drastically. (Even today, those who fire locomotives on preserved railways and on main-line rail tours still follow time-honoured traditions of locomotive preparation and firing technique.) A Gresley A1 carried eight tonnes of coal in the tender, together with 5,000 gallons of water, and these were the materials that created steam, when combined in the right manner. As locomotives developed the job of the fireman also became more taxing, as boilers became bigger and maximum boiler pressures were raised. In the early years of the twentieth century firemen were already being pushed hard physically as locomotives grew ever larger to meet the increasing demands that were placed on them. When *Flying Scotsman* first appeared there were concerns that the massive 41.5sq-ft firebox grate would be overwhelming for a single fireman, but it is a testament to their design that what these huge machines really required was skilled firemen to produce the right kind of fire, rather than sheer brute force.

Of course, firemen had to be fit. They would be on their feet for the majority of any journey, and travelling at speeds of up to 75mph – and more in some cases – required coal to be added to the fire almost continuously, so as to maintain working pressure. But that was just one of a fireman's tasks. At the same time he was responsible for managing the level of water in the boiler – too much, and the engine could prime and potentially damage the motion components; too little and disaster would hit the firebox and the crew on the footplate.

The water level always had to be above the level of the top of the firebox, which was encased within an outer casing of copper that joined the boiler, creating a single body full of water. Two gauge glasses and associated fittings were built into the back of a locomotive's firebox to measure this level and judge when more water was needed in the boiler. This was added using injectors, which combined water from the tender with steam from the boiler to literally inject fresh water into the boiler. With the water and the fire under control, a third job fell to the fireman – that of second man to the driver, providing a valuable second set of eyes to view the road ahead from the other side of the boiler barrel.

It was hot, dirty and heavy work that demanded physical strength and mental alertness. Route knowledge was essential to prepare for any steep climbs. It was no good starting at the bottom of a hill with a run-down fire to build on: a fireman had to be on top of his game and prepared for every eventuality. Shovel upon shovel of coal had to be moved from the tender, across the footplate to the firehole doors, and then it wasn't just a case of throwing the coal into any old place on the fire. The landing position of the coal is critical on a locomotive; it has to be skilfully placed in the correct areas of the fire, so as to evenly heat the whole firebox and avoid any holes developing in the firebed: quite simply a never-ending task.

The firebox of *Flying Scotsman* is typical of any large 'Pacific'. It is wide at the back with a small opening in the centre where the fireman feeds the coal, and that fuel has to reach the back corners of the firebox which are near-invisible when standing on the footplate. This is where the skill came in. It was a knack, something that could (and still can) be learned, and a true engineman would always know what to do. In practice it looks simple – a quick flick of the wrist as the shovel goes through the firehole door and you can hear the coal clunk into the corners of the firebox – but acquiring that knack and skill can take many hours of training and practice. The next hard part of keeping the fire going was reaching the front of the firebox some feet away. This did require some force, but it needed just as much skill as getting into the tricky back corners.

Drivers were often less than sympathetic towards their firemen. The driver had the power to make a fireman's life hell by driving hard and imposing strict rules about which half of the footplate was his and which half was the fireman's. There are many tales of drivers drawing an imaginary – or even real – line down the cab to keep the fireman where they wanted him. Former British Railways fireman Colin Churcher remembers one such incident:

Tom was one of the most miserable drivers I have ever met. He walked with a limp and had a permanent scowl on his face. To make matters worse, he was a short man and carried a piece of wood with him which he would place on his seat so that he could see out.

Tom made quite a name for himself among the young, inexperienced firemen at the depot, and everyone dreaded having to go with him. Everyone except Ray, that is. Ray was a quiet man who knew his job, but he had one basic fault. He could not fire from the right-hand side. On the 2-6-4 Ts the fireman had to move the coal from the bunker on his left to the firehole, which was on his right. This was the wrong way around for Ray who would fire with his back to the driver and from the driver's side.

One day Ray was booked to work a passenger train with Tom. They started out fine – that is until Ray started to fire from Tom's side of the cab. Every time Ray took a shovelful of coal he put his backside right into Tom's face (remember that Tom was a short man). This annoyed Tom so much that every time Ray went to swing the shovel, Tom poked him in the rear. Of course, this did not go down too well with Ray, and very soon they had an argument. At this, Tom climbed down from his seat, produced a piece of chalk and drew a line down the middle of the swaying footplate. He said to Ray, pointing to the two halves of the cab: 'That half is your half. This half is mine. You stick to your half, and I'll stick to mine'.

Similarly the footplate had to be kept tidy. Any coal that fell on to the cab floor had to be removed, and the footplate would often be washed down with water. The fireman's job was complicated further by the fact that different drivers had different ways of driving. There were drivers who were heavy on the regulator, meaning that, just like in a car when you push your foot to the floor, more fuel was used and more needed to be fed to the fire – by the fireman of course. It could be back-breaking work, and there was certainly no rest, even at stations, as again the fire would need tending to in the few short minutes spent standing at the platforms waiting for the guard's whistle.

On shed the fireman's jobs were many. Churcher explains his duties as a fireman in the 1950s:

The railway found that the morning turns were the most difficult to cover, and so most of my turns were morning ones. I would get up around 2.00 a.m., wash and make my breakfast. It was a short walk in the dark to book on at 3.00 a.m. I had to cross the loco yard which was dangerous. There was a thick pall of sulphurous smoke from the many banked fires which obscured the occasional light. One had to avoid the numerous piles of still-glowing cinders and keep an ear open to give a wide berth to any locomotive that was being worked on. The sound of fire irons signalled that one was likely to receive a shovelful of hot coals right in the face. In the background there would be the sounds of a locomotive being moved with open cylinder cocks and a very watery exhaust while the occasional wheezing sound would indicate that a dead engine was being moved. To make it worse there were ash pits, signal wires and point rods to avoid.

Having booked on, there was normally a lull for a couple

of hours waiting to see if a fireman was not going to show. Around 5.30 a.m. I might be allotted a locomotive and would start to prepare it. Some firemen would be sneaky and arrive as the engine was ready to leave – having let somebody else prepare it.

Engine preparation followed very much a standard routine. First check the water level and firebox. Crack the blower, throw over the fire, which had been banked under the firedoors, and build up the firebed. Check the coal and water supplies, lamps and other tools. These were in very short supply, and I frequently had to steal items from other engines. Once obtained, they would not leave my sight until the shed signal had been passed.

While I was raising steam and checking the smokebox and ashpan, my mate would be oiling round and inspecting the motion. Every driver had a pocket bulging with corks that were used to plug the oil reservoirs. Most would ensure the injectors were working properly. This was the fireman's responsibility but the driver would want to satisfy himself that this vital piece of equipment was functioning satis-factorily.

At the end of the day's shift out on the line, the fireman still had a great many jobs to do. After arriving at the terminus station and the end of shift, the driver and fireman would take a locomotive back to the shed. Then, having found a pit to work over, the job of cleaning the fire would begin. Colin Churcher continues:

The idea was to remove the clinkers that had formed over the firebars and to leave in the live coals ready for the next trip. For this the railway devised instruments of torture known as long and short slices and long and short pricker bars. A slice is a long-handled shovel used to remove the clinker. Also required were some cotton waste and a bucket of water to cool off one's hands and to douse small fires.

The normal procedure was to move the live coals forward (towards the smokebox) with the short slice to expose the clinker in the back part of the firebox. This would be broken up with the short pricker bar and removed with the slice by shovelling out through the firehole, through the cab and on to the ground. The live clinkers would inevitably start fires on the wooden cab floor, which would then be extinguished with the bucket of water. The long slice would then be used to move the live coals under the firehole, and the clinker at the front would be removed, again through the firehole. This was the most difficult part, as the slice was 8–10ft long, and the clinker had to be lifted over the live coals. Some would be difficult to break up into small enough pieces to go through the firehole, and occasionally part of the brick arch would fall during a trip and fuse to the firebars. The fire irons would heat up and become soft and useless. A battered slice could be improved by running the engine over the edge of the blade to straighten it!

With the fire cleaned, it was a moment's work to shovel in a bank of coal under the doors which would then keep alight for several hours. It was a less arduous task to clean out the ashpan and the smokebox, but one had to know which way the wind was blowing. Steam engines invariably had drips of hot water which would find the back of one's neck with uncanny accuracy, and the plastic grease-top cap came in very useful.

Locomotive disposal was the worst part of the fireman's job, and one can imagine my feelings one evening, when I had cleaned and banked my fire only to discover that the engine was due for a boiler washout, and the fire should have been just thrown out. The only good thing about throwing out the coal that I had just put in was that I was paid overtime for doing it!

The fireman's life was one of dirt and filth that came with working on steam locomotives. Everywhere you went in a steam shed there would be black surfaces tainted by the colour of coal. The footplate was dirty and hot, and the conditions in the sheds were not much better, with windows coated in grime and coal dust, and the floor similarly treated. But, at the same time, working on the railway in the days of steam brought with it a sense of pride. At one time it was every boy's dream to become an engine driver, and in reality that dream included becoming a fireman first.

If the fireman had it tough, he could take comfort in the fact that he shared the bouncing, draughty, dirty, hot environment of the footplate with his driver. As with firing, becoming an express locomotive driver was a long path, and often newly qualified drivers would find themselves working alongside newly qualified firemen on lesser duties, such as shunting in goods yards, or on local freight and passenger trains. The driver's job was physically easier than the fireman's, though many took a turn on the shovel to give their fireman a break, as well as some experience on the regulator. It was demanding mentally, though, requiring absolute concentration on the locomotive, the line ahead, signals and, of course, time. To do this for hours at a time takes a special kind of man, and only the very best were allowed to drive the toughest freight and passenger trains.

It seems odd, in the face of today's youth-obsessed society, that the drivers who broke the speed records were all in their fifties, and looked nothing like the daredevil speed demons flying aeroplanes at the time. But, while test pilots needed cat-like reflexes and fearlessness, the express engine driver needed experience. He had to know every kink in the track, every curve, every hill, every approach to every station, where the signals and signal boxes were, and the speed limits too. On top of that, he also had to know how to handle his train in conditions from snow and ice to the track-buckling heat of summer. Trying to drive a train really fast without this knowledge was to court disaster, and, sensibly, the railways kept to their tried-and-tested ways.

Drivers could be very different. On the one hand, drivers like William Sparshatt, who took *Flying Scotsman* into the record books, were known as 'hard hitters' – men prepared to drive fast irrespective of coal consumption and their fireman. Though these men set records, they were also expensive on coal, and depended on having a top-notch fireman who could keep pace with their efforts. At the other end of the spectrum were drivers who sought to do no more than keep to time, and use as little coal as possible. It was a tricky balancing act, and every depot had drivers who found it difficult to keep time, just as they had hard-hitters. The responsibility of the driver was total, and the best espoused absolute professionalism, drinking in moderation and taking their job seriously, often spending time in the mutual improvement classes set up by the railways to train less experienced hands. In many ways, they were the elite of the working class, and their children were expected to do well in school, such was the status of their fathers.

It's very different these days. Modern trains are becoming increasingly complex, and train companies use advanced simulators to train staff and help them learn routes. Endurance and stamina now take second place to concentration, memory and technique – and rightly so, because it's generally acknowledged that driving a train is as demanding as flying an airliner. Yet, despite the differences, the essential qualities needed to be a train driver remain, and the top-link drivers of the LNER would doubtless have relished the chance to drive modern electric trains over the East Coast Main Line for mile after mile at 125mph.

These were the glamour jobs – the ones every schoolboy wanted – but there were plenty of others too. The experience of C.A. Scarboro, a restaurant car attendant on the London to Leeds run, is typical. Each person required fourteen pieces of silver and five pieces of crockery laying out before orders were collected and recorded, after which the attendants faced the challenge of serving food and drink on a bouncing, galloping train. On one occasion, Scarboro dropped a hot pot of tea over a passenger's leg. After making what he called 'the best job' of the situation, he was told he'd chosen the wrong limb to drop it on as its companion was artificial!

Working on the trains, however demanding, was a piece of cake compared with some jobs – A.F. Harris was a coalman at an engine shed in Essex, and his job was to hand-coal the locomotives at his shed. He reckoned that between himself and his colleague, they shovelled twenty-six tonnes of coal per day, by shovel and (for the larger lumps) by hand; and this man only weighed 9st 5lb!

There were countless other unsung heroes on the railway: the timetable clerks and engineering staff; the porters and typists; signalmen and shunters, wheel-tappers and boiler-smiths. All had one thing in common: they worked long, hard hours, often for very little pay, to keep the trains running.

But, as far as the public was concerned, it was the drivers who were the stars. Men like Sparshatt and Duddington (driver of the 126mph *Mallard*) became celebrities, at least as respected as sportsmen of the day. The travelling public knew their job was a hard one, with great responsibility, and gave engine crew appropriate respect. If the firemen can be regarded as the craftsmen of the steam age, and the engines the performers, the drivers were the artists. Their hands playing regulator and reverser against each other, they, more than any other group, played out the symphony of steam for more than a century.

Chapter Six
End of an Era

Gresley died in April 1941, ill and exhausted. But he could look back at a career that from gentle beginnings at the London & North Western Railway had taken him into the pantheon of engineering greats, along with the likes of Brunel, Stephenson and Churchward. His locomotives and carriages had set standards that would remain unbeaten for decades.

But the world had changed massively since the formation of the LNER in 1923. Then, big, complicated express locomotives and trains could be justified on the grounds of prestige and the availability of cheap, plentiful labour to staff, maintain and service them. But in 1941 Britain's ability to sustain its struggle against Germany was being tested to the limit, thanks to the depredations of the U-Boats, and those big, complicated express locomotives and luxury trains were starting to look just that: big, complicated luxuries at a time when Britain needed every locomotive, carriage and wagon in service to help the war effort. All four railway companies were in a more or less similar situation – too many locomotives requiring too much maintenance at a time when the nation could least afford it – but the LNER was probably in a worse situation than the others, not helped by its lack of cash.

It was a difficult time for the railways, as it was for everyone else. The war effort took priority over all other traffic, and even the railways were denuded of all but the bare minimum of support staff. On the outbreak of war, the government took control of the railways for the duration, and almost immediately many locomotives were painted black to help camouflage them. The apple-green express livery of the LNER was simply too visible from the air, particularly at night. This simple move immediately emphasised the urgency of the situation and, combined with the blackout, meant that pre-war glamour had given way to outright practicality. The streamlined trains so popular before the war were now essentially useless, and the carriages were stored, as was much of the A4 locomotive fleet for a while.

It didn't take long for someone to recognise that storing such powerful locomotives was an act of folly, irrespective of whether it looked appropriate or not to run a streamlined locomotive on less prestigious passenger, mail and even goods trains. With traffic demands at a high and growing throughout the war, spare locomotives were at a premium, and if the only locomotive available for a freight train was one of Gresley's sublime Pacifics, so be it.

Freight and troop movements understandably took priority over all other traffic, and this, combined with a maximum speed limit of 60mph imposed on all passenger trains, meant that for those civilian passengers who had to travel journeys became much harder. Many stations had their name boards removed in a bid to thwart German spies, such were the security concerns at the time. But this was only the beginning of the difficulties: with so many military personnel travelling all over the country, passenger trains were packed with people, and the chances of getting a seat were minimal. Generally, though, people tolerated the difficulties well, conscious of the war effort.

When one considers that before the war a long passenger train might have had twelve coaches or so, the lengths of some trains during the war beggared belief. The record, it seems, goes to one of twenty-six coaches hauled out of King's Cross by a Gresley V2. That was exceptional, but it certainly wasn't unknown for the locomotives on passenger trains leaving King's Cross to be in Gasworks Tunnel (the tunnel visible from the station platforms) before departure.

For engine crews, the war brought a host of new challenges. The need to sustain the blackout meant that many locomotives had side windows plated over, and on tender engines, awkward blackout sheets were fitted, which were supposed to stretch between cab and tender (the glow of a firebox at night representing a tantalising target of opportunity for a roaming Luftwaffe pilot with bullets and bombs to spare).

Operating conditions became worse as well. Simple things like fire irons and tools became scarce, with many crews having to steal them from other locomotives. Locomotives were cleaned less frequently and were often kept in service in a condition that before the war would have seen them sent for overhaul and repair. It didn't help that parts of the main locomotive works at least were turned over to military production — meaning that, over time, a maintenance backlog developed. On top of this, trains were often delayed by hours because of congestion and failure; crews could be on the footplate for twelve hours at a time – long enough for a non-stop run from London to Aberdeen with 1890s timings – so bad was the situation.

After Gresley's death in 1941 the LNER board appointed as his successor the man they considered best able to deliver the rolling stock the company needed at the lowest cost in capital, labour and ongoing maintenance; what was needed in wartime wasn't a brilliant vision, it was practical, down-to-earth engineering competence. The man they chose was the carriage and wagon superintendent, Edward Thompson, by now aged sixty. He was a good choice, as witnessed by his work in the carriage and wagon department, and it was a logical promotion for which he'd waited a long time. Even so, eighteen years after his father-in-law Vincent Raven had been passed over for the post of Chief Mechanical Engineer in favour of Gresley, Thompson still hadn't forgiven his predecessor.

On arrival at Doncaster, one of the first things he is reputed to have said to his senior team is: 'I have a lot to do and very little time to do it.' Clearly, things were going to change a lot. They needed to. The availability and reliability of Gresley's big express locomotives, the V2s, the A1 and A3 Pacifics, and the streamlined A4s, was by now starting to become a major concern. All four designs were performing prodigious feats, hauling trains of lengths and weights far beyond anything Gresley could have imagined, but they were failing too often. Thompson laid the blame for this squarely on the conjugated valve gear so beloved of Gresley. He was probably right too.

Though certain railway occupations, such as engine crew and many engineering roles, were exempt from conscription (they were known as reserved occupations), other jobs, such as cleaning, invariably fell by the wayside owing to staff shortages and the rush to get engines into service. For the conjugated valve gear, this lack of cleaning proved little short of disastrous. Gresley had placed its levers in front of the cylinders to make maintenance and adjustment easier, but there was a catch: the assembly was vulnerable to smokebox ash falling out of the front of the locomotive during routine maintenance. Smokebox ash is formed of the particles of burned and unburned coal that are light enough to be carried through the boiler by the hot gases from the firebox but too heavy to be carried through the chimney. After a day's work it was not unknown for a smokebox to be half-full of this ash, which was fine, like a rough sand, and extremely sharp; if any that landed on the plating in front of the smokebox wasn't cleaned off thoroughly after the smokebox was emptied, it could, and would, find its way everywhere, including into the precisely installed motion that drove the valves for the middle cylinder of the conjugated valve gear.

These sharp particles increased the wear on the valve gear, and the lack of regular tender loving care in the running sheds only exacerbated the problem. Something, felt Thompson, needed to be done. There were sceptics about his view even in 1941, but it's difficult to see what choice he really had at the time. Nobody knew how long the war would last, or what conditions would be like if and when it was won. The conjugated valve gear was a major cause for operational concern, and something needed to be done to improve it.

While he was considering his options on this, Thompson was also preparing a 'go-anywhere' mixed-traffic locomotive design along the lines of similar types introduced by the other 'Big Four' companies. It would be simple and powerful, with wide availability and great attention paid to ease of maintenance; aesthetics and speed would have to come second if necessary. Thompson's first design, the B1 4-6-0, was an instant hit, proving itself both powerful and fast, and looking chunky yet elegant into the bargain. It was built into the 1950s, and was one of the last steam types to remain in service, running until 1967.

It took time for Thompson to decide what to do about the conjugated valve gear, and, with victory looming from about 1943 (not to mention an influx of cheaply built heavy freight locomotives from the USA and Britain's own independent locomotive builders reducing the need to run passenger locomotives on unsuitable duties), he started to consider what the next generation of express passenger locomotives should be. Under his new philosophy, maximum use would be made of standard components, such as connecting rods, with little room for variation.

Thompson, like many engineers, preferred to split the load of the cylinders, with the outside pair driving on to the middle coupled axle, and the middle cylinder driving on the leading coupled axle. This design, known as 'divided drive', reduced the stress imposed on the middle crank axle, and, with the wheels coupled in any case, would have no practical effect on the amount of grip a locomotive could exert. However, Thompson's somewhat extreme policy of conformity meant that he decided to move the inside cylinder forward and provide a separate set of valve gear for it. This would make maintenance more time-consuming but simpler, and so would increase reliability.

Of course, he had to prove his theory, and funds were too tight to allow him to do it with a new locomotive; he would have to rebuild first. He chose his victims carefully, starting in 1943 with the graceful and elegant P2 2-8-2s used on the onerous Edinburgh–Aberdeen run. These beautiful machines, which presaged the art-deco streamlining used on the peerless A4s, and whose wheel arrangement gave them tremendous grip as well as speed, were converted into ungainly Pacifics that simply looked wrong. Moving the middle cylinder forward forced Thompson to stretch the front end, and the location of the new bogie saw the outside cylinders look much further backwards than on Gresley's designs. Then he went further still, converting a quartet of the magnificent V2 2-6-2s on the production line into an even odder-looking bunch of locomotives. With their smaller boilers, they looked as if the builders had run short of metal.

The critics were horrified by the aesthetics of these hybrid rebuilds, and even now there's unquestionably something extremely odd about their look. It might be the huge expanse of empty space at the lower front when viewed side-on, or the fact that they had to be stretched to accommodate Thompson's standardisation policy, but either way, they made a poor showing in comparison with the grace and elegance perpetuated by Gresley, and before him Ivatt.

Thompson by now had the bit well and truly between his teeth, and in a bid to deface Gresley's proud legacy did something that in retrospect seems as sacrilegious as turning HMS *Victory* into a rowing boat. He wanted to convert an A1 into one of his new 'standard' Pacifics to showcase his design, and he could have chosen any of eighteen locomotives for this (including *Flying Scotsman*). Yet, in an act of calculated destruction, he chose the pioneer of them all, the first-born, *Great Northern* herself.

She emerged from works in September 1945, and the shockwaves can still be felt if you look at a picture. Gone was the neat layout of yore, with curved splashers covering the tops of the wheels and the outside cylinders nesting neatly halfway between the wheels of the front bogie. With her cylinders set well back, and the smokebox extended, she almost looked as if the front end of a different engine had been bolted on to her. In some senses, it had been. Going back, the extension of the cab sidesheets to meet the bottom of the firebox and tender was gone, leaving it perched precariously, the critics argued. I think *Great Northern* actually looked quite purposeful and modern in her first rebuilt form, but the directors of the LNER evidently took a different view, as before long she had her appearance tweaked, with cabs similar to the other express engines, and smoke-deflecting sheets at the sides of the smokebox. Visually, these alterations made Thompson's rebuild look like a dog's dinner. It's ironic, and possibly deliberate, that these rebuilds looked so ugly compared with Thompson's B1 design. His desire, nurtured for years, to eliminate Gresley's legacy was nothing short of outright desecration.

If *Great Northern*'s performances had been transformed to, say, the levels reached by the A4 fleet in tip-top condition, but with greater reliability, then Thompson's rebuilding might have been defensible, just. It wasn't. *Great Northern*, like all of Thompson's rebuilds, failed to get close to the performances recorded by the A3s and A4s, and didn't offer good-enough reliability to compensate. It is no coincidence that of all the LNER's Pacifics, it was Thompson's which were withdrawn first. Thankfully, Thompson's ability to inflict further damage on the Pacific fleet was limited by his retirement in 1946. *Flying Scotsman* remained intact as an A1, while Thompson's successor, Arthur Peppercorn, set about trying to limit the damage.

Great Northern, and petty vindictiveness aside, though, it's difficult to see what options Thompson had regarding Gresley's designs during wartime, given the uncertainty about the future, and particularly the conjugated valve gear. After the war had been won, however, there was no need for rebuilding an A1 – particularly as, by Thompson's own admission, the remaining A1s, converted into the more powerful A3s, would still have had many years of life ahead of them. His mistake, it seems, was to move the inside cylinder forward to drive on the leading coupled wheels. If he had left them driving the middle pair, his alterations might have worked.

In 1946 *Flying Scotsman* was roughly halfway through her life, and still in her original form. Her once record-breaking performance was now regarded as everyday, and she was just another member of the largest stable of Pacifics in Britain. After the trauma of Thompson, his successor was preparing designs for what he intended to be the final generation of express steam locomotives on the East Coast Main Line before the introduction of a fleet of diesel locomotives, and then eventual electrification.

Peppercorn, a heart-and-soul Great Northern man, agreed with Thompson about splitting the drive between the leading and middle coupled axle, but he disagreed profoundly about having to have all the coupling rods of the same length. By using shorter components than for the outside cylinders, he was able to eliminate the need to lengthen the locomotives, benefiting their appearance.

At a time when the Doncaster design staff was already expressing concern about Thompson's design of front end, Peppercorn must have been welcomed with sighs of relief. In 1947 Gresley's A1 design was reclassified A10. Peppercorn's A1 design was entirely new and perhaps the most modern in the country at the time. Thompson's final Pacific design, the A2, was revised in the light of Peppercorn's and Doncaster preferences, and eventually became extremely successful. Peppercorn's A1 was a true successor to *Flying Scotsman* and her brethren. Fast, powerful, and exceedingly reliable, it was finally to prove to be the design that could displace many of the A3s to other routes which were crying out for high-quality express passenger locomotives.

At the outbreak of war in 1939, the government had promised to cover the cost of rehabilitating the railways after victory, but in 1945 there was a different government with entirely different motives. Clement Attlee had been elected on a socialist mandate and promised widespread reform, from the introduction of a national health service to improved education and, crucially, nationalisation of the industries which had worked so well under government supervision (if not control) during the war. Conveniently, the 1922 Railways Act had made provision for nationalisation of the Big Four twenty-five years later – in 1948.

Initial attempts to speed up train services after the war were hit by the state of the track, which really made the high-80s and 90mph speeds of the 1930s impossible until repairs were undertaken. Even so, the LNER reintroduced many of its named trains in a bid to try to improve morale, the theory being that, even if journey times were still extraordinarily long, passengers would feel happier about the train if it was named. Whether it worked or not is unrecorded.

In 1947, almost twenty-five years after she emerged from Doncaster Works, *Flying Scotsman* was finally modified into an A3. Her old 180psi boiler was replaced by a more powerful 225psi version, and her cylinders and valves were replaced with the more efficient types developed in the light of the 1925 locomotive exchange with the Great Western. Now more powerful than ever, she received her final number in LNER ownership, the anonymous 103.

Chapter Seven
The Fires Go Out

With the advent of nationalisation, rationalisation of Britain's railways also began. First, with the introduction of the British Railways Standard steam locomotives, there was a cull of pre-nationalisation locomotive designs, but more drastic changes were needed to keep the railway as a useful transport asset and to contend with the rapidly expanding road network.

Private car ownership was beginning to rise, and to compete with the comfort, rail had to be faster and more luxurious. New coaches called 'BR Mk 1' began to appear from 1954, but it was 1955 that saw perhaps the most important change to the railways, in the Modernisation Plan. Under this plan BR would spend £1,240 million on new diesel locomotives to rid the network of dirty, ageing and increasingly expensive steam power. Similarly, freight traffic was being lost to the roads, and the railway needed new designs to compete with lorries.

The writing was on the wall for steam, but, thanks to a handful of dedicated and progressive staff, steam's performances were set to get even better. The charge was led by a brilliant young shedmaster called Peter Townend, who in 1956 became the youngest boss of King's Cross's prestigious 'Top Shed', the London home of the East Coast's stable of racehorses.

Townend, born in 1925, had enjoyed a swift rise through the ranks and, after impressing his seniors with his enthusiasm and ability, landed one of the toughest tasks on the railway – sorting out the problems at Top Shed. In 1956 it's no exaggeration to say that this critical piece of the maintenance jigsaw had serious problems. Reliability of its fleet was collapsing, and there were real questions being asked of it after its usual allocation of 19 A4s and 12 A3s was increased to 42 Pacifics, once through working to Newcastle and Leeds was introduced (previously, engines were changed en route). There were also problems of racism, with whites and 'coloureds' unbelievably having separate mess rooms. Townend had one hell of a challenge.

He rose to it with enthusiasm, first sorting out the bearing problems that the streamlined A4s had suffered since the fleet was introduced in the 1930s. Thanks to taking a personal interest in the work being undertaken at the shed, he was able to increase the mileages being worked by the locomotives between failures from their previous low levels to some of the highest anywhere in Britain. It was a remarkable turnaround, and it continued because Townend wanted to improve the steaming of his locomotives.

In the 1950s most of the really good coal being mined in Britain was exported to earn precious foreign exchange, and that meant that industry, including the railways, had to make do with what was left. Much of this coal was pretty awful stuff, and, though the worst was reserved for freight locomotives, a lot of it didn't burn as hot as the coal the Gresley Pacifics had enjoyed before the war. This meant that, in order to keep up with steam demand, more coal had to be shovelled on, adding to running costs. With a poor load of coal, even the best crews would struggle to get the most out of their charge.

But Townend, along with other colleagues on the former Great Western, knew that if you could urge the fire to burn harder, you could extract every bit of heat out of it, and make the most of the potential performance of the locomotive. The secret lay with the blastpipe and chimney, part of the 'front end'. The blastpipe was the outlet for the steam exhausted from the cylinders, and as this steam went up and out of the chimney it dragged hot gases from the fire with it. The theory was simple: the faster you could get these exhaust gases moving, the more air they would draw through the boiler and firegrate, and the hotter the fire would burn. There would, in engineering terms, be less back-pressure on the hot gases leaving the firebox. There were a number of ways of achieving this, and all worked on the principle of splitting the flow of this exhaust gas in order to increase its surface area so it could draw more air with it. What Townend wanted to do was hardly original. One of the decisive contributory factors to *Mallard*'s record-breaking run in 1938 had been its special exhaust arrangement – known as 'Kylchap', after its designers (Kylälä, from Finland, and the French locomotive genius André Chapelon), which was a popular way of increasing power.

Initially – and unsurprisingly, as British Railways was a

state-owned company – his request to fit Kylchap exhausts to his fleet was refused on grounds of cost, but Townend persisted. He knew that by fitting them to the A3 and A4 Pacifics and as many others as possible not only would performance improve, but coal consumption would fall too. In 1959 *Flying Scotsman* was fitted with a Kylchap exhaust and the double chimney needed to accommodate it. The cost was just £153 per locomotive, and with coal savings of 6lbs to 7lbs per mile, it doesn't take an accountant to work out that the railways very quickly made a profit on their expenditure.

It's ironic that in the twilight of their lives, performance of the A3s had finally reached its potential. To all intents and purposes, on all but the most demanding of duties, they were every bit the equal of the A4s. So much so that they returned to use on the prestigious titled trains to Newcastle and back, working duties of up to 546 miles a day with a turnaround time at Newcastle of just 55 minutes. By the standards of the day, this was a railway operating with the precision of a Swiss watch.

Townend, Top Shed and his Pacifics should have been given the next decade to prove their worth, but, as dieselisation gathered pace, the days of Top Shed and its Pacifics were numbered. Nobody knew quite when the axe would fall, but it was now a question of 'when' rather than 'if'. Time was running out.

The first British diesel locomotives were used for shunting, initially with the LMS before the Second World War. In fact it was the LMS, the LNER's great rival, that pioneered the use of powerful diesel locomotives for main-line passenger services with a pair of locomotives built at Derby Works in 1947. These paved the way for future locomotives, but one in particular would cause the death of steam on the East Coast Main Line race track. Called *Deltic*, she was the most powerful diesel locomotive in the world at the time and she was also light and fast. Extensive trials showed that diesel traction could make a major difference to the speed and performance of trains, although *Deltic* herself was felt to be too expensive to build, and too time-consuming to maintain. When her engine failed, she was withdrawn from service.

Though British Railways was still building steam locomotives, in 1958 the first products of the ill-conceived modernisation plan were tentatively entering traffic, and unsurprisingly the East Coast Main Line was first in line to receive them. Known as English Electric Type 4s, these had a 2,000-horsepower engine and should have been able to put Gresley's steam locomotives in the shade, because on an average day an A3 like *Flying Scotsman* (now at her final shed at King's Cross) was able to put out around 1,500hp. But it wasn't quite as simple as that. While all the power *Flying Scotsman* was able to generate went from the boiler to the pistons to the wheels, that 2,000hp output of the diesels was absorbed, bit by bit, by onboard electrics and the generator used to power the electric motors that drove the wheels. So much so that, when it came to the power that reached the rail, these new diesels were only able to lay down 1,550hp – no more, in practical terms, than the locomotives they were designed to replace.

With the Type 4s unable to reach the potential required for the East Coast Main Line services, BR turned back to the Deltic concept. Between 1961 and 1962 the fleet of twenty-two locomotives carrying numbers D9000-D9022 entered traffic, slowly relegating steam to lesser duties and restricting it to certain areas. These 3,300hp, 100mph diesels had impressive characteristics for the early 1960s and rapidly revolutionised railway services on the East Coast Main Line both for the passengers and the crews. With the increase in speeds, infrastructure was also upgraded to reduce journey times between major cities.

The cab of a diesel was a world away from the dirty, hot and uncomfortable confines of a steam locomotive footplate. Now the driver needed to have a heater in the cab for colder months, but he also got much better vision, a comfortable chair, windscreen wipers and, most importantly, a clean atmosphere in which to work. The controls were much simpler to follow, and in some ways (although driving a train is never easy) much easier to operate. Now, rather than having to coax the best out of a locomotive, the diesel power units and electric traction motors did the physical work for the driver, and power could be increased virtually at the touch of a button, rather than through preparation of the fire and boiler pressure.

It was a new and bold era, where diesel designs were being tried and tested in service to evaluate performance. The irony was that the Modernisation Plan effectively wasted money just as much as the final years of the steam locomotive construction programme, because yet more money was spent on diesel designs that didn't reach the desired potential, leading to their early withdrawal. Some designs fared much better and became the staple of the British Railways motive power fleet, and even today there are locomotives that originated in the early 1960s continuing in service on the main line, admirably doing the job they were built for. With the dawn of the Modernisation Plan, however, the future was bleak for steam, and *Flying Scotsman*.

Chapter Eight
Knight in Shining Armour

I n 1924 the wealthy owners of the Northern Rubber company in Retford took their four-year-old son to the Wembley exhibition. Though he must have been dazzled by the exhibits, one stood out above all others: the apple-green *Flying Scotsman*.

'I gazed up at this huge gleaming machine and was lifted into its cab. I remember being impressed at how clean it was compared with the grimier engines we saw at home, and how marvellous its apple-green paint was compared with the smaller engine alongside it [*Caerphilly Castle*]. I was spell-bound, and couldn't stop thinking about it all the way home,' he recalled in an interview in *The Railway Magazine*.

As he grew up, Alan Pegler got to know the staff at his nearest station, Barnby Moor, and became a keen and extremely proficient photographer. He certainly wasn't a shrinking violet, and thanks to his family's wealth got a private pilot's licence when he was just seventeen. To nobody's surprise, the young Pegler used it to chase trains from the air: always, of course, his beloved LNER. The impact made by *Flying Scotsman* in the 1920s still loomed large over this young man.

Wartime brought a posting to the Fleet Air Arm, and, thanks to his private pilot's licence, Pegler became a pilot flying Skua dive-bombers. Appendicitis curtailed his flying career, but he transferred to the Royal Observer Corps, which he was involved in throughout the 1950s and 1960s. It was after the war that Pegler's wanderlust came to the fore. In late 1946, he was demobilised and went back to Retford and Northern Rubber. The company had no links with railways, but Pegler's office window overlooked the Sheffield-to-Lincoln railway; his passion for railways, dormant since the war, started to return. His duties at Northern Rubber were far from taxing, as the company largely ran itself, and he had a good income and time on his hands, but it wasn't until he travelled on a special train run by British Railways to mark the centenary of the Great Northern Railway's main line in 1950 that his enthusiasm for the railway really reignited.

In 1950 it was Northern Rubber's eightieth anniversary, and Pegler decided he would plan an excursion for the company's staff. This wasn't a particularly unusual thing to do back then: plenty of big companies organised day trips for their staff, and the railways, always keen to make more money, had been happy to accommodate them. The first of Pegler's specials ran from Retford to London in May 1951 to take staff to the Festival of Britain. Further excursions saw him taking former LNER locomotives to destinations as far away as Blackpool: the staff must have loved him. Pegler had by now well and truly got the railway bug back.

At this point, Pegler was little more than a generous employer taking his staff on trips. In September 1952, though, he did something really unusual. In conjunction with a friend, Trevor Bailey, he arranged with the Eastern Region of British Railways to run a special train to celebrate the centenary of the line between Retford, Newark and Grantham. On 28 September a train hauled by A4 60007 *Sir Nigel Gresley* (also known as 4498) took 400 railway enthusiasts to the old railway museum (the current National Railway Museum opened only in the 1970s) in York. It was a rare thing back then – a special, chartered train where bookings were open to the public. It was a complete contrast with the private specials run by companies, and it heralded the proper start of today's charter train business.

Pegler had a ready market for these trips. He was president of the Gainsborough Model Railway Society, one of the pre-eminent organisations of its type in the country at the time. Alan Burton joined the society in 1949 aged eleven: 'It was quite exciting – I'd just been given my very first model. I didn't know anybody to start with, but everybody was of a like mind, and I was one of the young "erks". We were told Alan Pegler had been named President, and this big rosy-faced chap walked in – he was one of those people who lights up a room the moment he walks in.'

A year later, Pegler really surpassed himself by persuading the powers-that-be on the Eastern Region to remove two historic locomotives from the York Museum – two old Great Northern Railway 'Atlantics' – restore them to working order, and use them to double-head a train from King's Cross to Doncaster to celebrate the centenary of the famous Doncaster Works where *Flying Scotsman* was built.

Five hundred enthusiasts crammed the first train, and it was so popular that a second train ran from Leeds to London a week later.

For Burton and lads like himself, it was almost too much: 'It was quite something. I can remember not sleeping at night getting ready for it: it was a huge adventure! And for a twelve-year old boy to be part of that train, because our guvnors were running it, to get on it when all those people were watching – I felt a million dollars!' (So old were these two locomotives that Burton and the dozen or so youngsters in the society were astonished to find they weren't even listed in their spotting books.) The trains attracted huge publicity, to the pleasant surprise of the Eastern Region's bosses, and the gobsmacked excitement of enthusiasts along its entire route.

The stage was set for Pegler to run more charters, and with official blessing too. Specials began to run all over the country, taking people like Alan Burton to parts of the country they would never otherwise have seen. Pegler loved it, and seemingly enjoyed having the money to do it: 'It was something different,' says Burton, 'it was like a big toy for him, and I never saw him unhappy on the trains.'

One of the passengers on Pegler's charters was a buffet-car steward who regularly served the deputy chairman of the British Transport Commission, Sir John Benstead, on a morning train from Grantham to King's Cross. The steward's enthusiasm for these special trains must have proved contagious, because Benstead recommended Pegler to BTC Chairman Sir Brian Robertson for a place on a newly established regional board. British Railways, it seemed, was delighted that Pegler was giving the Eastern Region such a positive public image, so Sir Brian agreed, and, even though Pegler was seventeen years younger than any other member, he was offered a place as a part-time member of the Eastern Area board. 'It was astonishing really . . . complete luck!' enthused Pegler, who had finally succeeded in making a career out of the railway.

Before his appointment, however, Pegler had already been busy on an altogether different kind of railway in distant Wales. Around the world, railways with narrower tracks have long been popular, as they allow tighter curves to be built, and require less substantial engineering to construct and maintain. In Britain, because standard-gauge railways were already so well-established, narrow-gauge lines only really gained a foothold in the mountainous area of North Wales, where the need to transport huge quantities of slate from the mountain quarries to ports had seen a number of them established.

By the early 1950s, just a couple were in operation: one, from Aberystwyth to Devil's Bridge, was owned by British Railways. The other, from Tywyn to Abergynolwyn, was owned privately, and was on its last legs. A daring attempt to operate the latter (known as the Talyllyn Railway) as a volunteer-run tourist attraction had started in 1951, and a chance conversation between one of its pioneers, Lord Northesk, and Pegler on the July centenary train in 1950 saw Pegler gravitate inexorably to the Ffestiniog Railway, which ran from Porthmadog to Blaenau Ffestiniog. This, asserted

Northesk, was the line the Talyllyn volunteers had *really* wanted to restore. To a man like Pegler, the challenge was irresistible.

This 13.5-mile line had been built in the nineteenth century to transport slate (and later passengers), and it's said that this picturesque, sinuous and hilly route helped roof the empire. It had a gauge of a fraction under two feet (compared with the standard gauge of 4ft 8.5in.) but was far from a toy railway. The war had taken its toll, though, and with little of the tourist traffic on which it had come to depend, and with quarries turning to lorries, the line had closed in August 1946, with track, engines and carriages abandoned where they lay. Pegler visited it in 1952, and nothing had changed.

> It was a decrepit, decaying, derelict shambles. What on earth induced us to think it was worth having a go I'll never know, especially as several other prospective purchasers had already run a mile from it – but you have to remember that it wasn't long after the war, and young men like us were filled with a supreme blind optimism which made us believe we could make the world a better place.

The Ffestiniog was crippled with debts and complicated legal problems, which was why most prospective purchasers had withdrawn with their tails between their legs, but Pegler's friend Trevor Bailey had a brother-in-law, a solicitor called John Routley, who boasted that he could clear up any legal mess. Pegler threw down a challenge to Routley's professional pride by asking him to sort out the problems of the Ffestiniog, and Routley bit hook, line, and sinker. It quickly became apparent that Pegler's challenge would be a tough one, but two exhausting years after he started, Routley broke the news to Pegler that it would be possible to gain ownership of the railway, albeit at the cost of tens of thousands of pounds. It would also be possible to buy a controlling interest for the comparatively small sum of £3,000, but the problem with that was that it required a guarantee of a further £45,000 to succeed – a gigantic amount at the time! Pegler, with some trepidation, went to visit his father, the titular head of the Northern Rubber Company. He explained his plans and expected a tough time. His father, surely, would never back such a crazy project. Pegler Senior must have drawn a deep breath before saying to his son: 'You don't want to go paying bank charges young man   I'll give you an interest-free loan!'

Suddenly, Pegler's dream of reopening the old, almost forgotten Ffestiniog was alive and kicking. In June 1954 he gained his controlling interest, which he subsequently transferred to a charitable trust. It was the first railway line in Britain to have closed and then been reopened by railway enthusiasts (the pioneering Talyllyn was kept open, thanks to the early efforts of dedicated supporters). The Ffestiniog set the pattern for much of the preservation movement that was to follow, and it's thanks to Pegler's generosity, ingenuity, and outright passion that it reopened when it did. Not for nothing is Pegler regarded by many as the founding father of railway preservation.

Pegler took up his appointment on the Eastern Region Area Board in 1955, the year of the much-vaunted Modernisation Plan. It was an auspicious moment: railway enthusiasts were often greeted with suspicion by senior management, but in Pegler, they had inadvertently appointed *Flying Scotsman*'s greatest fan. Without his appointment to the area board, it now seems unlikely that *Flying Scotsman* would have survived; instead, she would have joined her sisters in the scrap line.

The distractions of the board, and of the Ffestiniog, which he would hold the chairmanship of until 1972, were diverting Alan Pegler too much from his day job at Northern Rubber however. He may well have been indulging in the railway equivalent of his father's passion for farming, but after his father died in 1957 the other members of the family became increasingly concerned that Pegler Junior wasn't spending enough time on the business. Peglers of Doncaster, a firm operated by another part of the family, finally took over Northern Rubber in 1961. Alan Pegler's share of the deal was £70,000 – equivalent to £500,000 or so today. He was still only forty-one, and had a fortune in his pocket.

By the early 1960s, steam was starting to leave the stage. The planned phased replacement of steam under the Modernisation Plan was becoming outright slaughter. Already, thousands of serviceable, economic locomotives had been sacrificed, and as the new diesels entered service the scrapman's hunger became a feeding frenzy. In 1947, the year before nationalisation, there had been around 20,000 steam locomotives in service on Britain's main-line railways (a figure that doesn't include the many thousands of locomotives used by industry). A decade later, there were still almost 17,000, although diesels were starting to make an impact in places, but that remaining 17,000 would all be gone by August 1968. It was extinction on a cataclysmic scale.

The first region to rid itself of steam power was the Western Region. Steeped in the tradition of the former Great Western Railway, the managers made an early decision to eradicate steam. After trials with two Gas Turbine locomotives in the early 1950s, the Region opted for diesel hydraulic locomotives, and by 1962, with a full complement of diesels available, the death knell sounded for steam on most of its lines. On the other side of the country the Eastern Region of BR (formerly the LNER) was also feeling the pinch, and with the introduction of the high-speed 100mph production 'Deltic' diesels in 1961, time was called on express steam designs, including the streamlined A4s and their A3 counterparts. The A3s were relegated to lesser duties or withdrawn, whilst the A4s received a stay of execution, hauling express trains between Edinburgh and Aberdeen. On the East Coast Main Line, though, steam was all but gone.

As diesels were introduced steam was gradually run down. Not just in numbers, but also in maintenance and cleaning. By 1960 steam locomotives were becoming sufficiently outmoded that maintenance was reduced; in some cases the mechanical condition was allowed to deteriorate, and external appearances certainly left a lot to be desired. Locomotives were now rarely cleaned. They still had a job to do, but their appearance certainly reflected the incoming tide of new diesels. The golden age of steam was truly over, and it was only a matter of time until steam was completely eradicated from main-line work. The first of *Flying Scotsman*'s sister engines, 60104 *Solario*, succumbed as early as 1959. (Incredibly, at that time British Railways was still building steam locomotives: the last, a heavy freight engine, wouldn't be built until 1960!)

Historically, when locomotives were withdrawn from service, they were scrapped by the railway itself at one of its locomotive works. Any parts that couldn't be re-used were melted down and turned into new locomotives. Now, though, the railway works – already at capacity, thanks to the diesel building programme – simply couldn't cope with this mass extinction. Queues of forlorn steam locomotives lined the sidings of places like Swindon, Doncaster, Crewe and Darlington, often with their connecting rods cut and their fires dead, awaiting their inevitable fate.

When the end came for a steam locomotive, it was never pretty. Not for these gallant machines the dignity of being disassembled into their component parts. It was brutal. Standing wherever they could, the scrapmen torched holes in the metalwork that had been so diligently formed, joined, maintained and operated over the years. Boiler tubes were severed like veins, the valve gear amputated, and the wheels gas-axed, all in the name of progress.

As withdrawals accelerated, private scrap merchants were encouraged to buy these old steam locomotives from British

Railways and scrap them themselves. Macabre cavalcades of dead steam locomotives moved to these scrapyards, often hauled by a locomotive also doomed to have its fire dropped in the scrapyard for the last time and then join the others in the scrap lines.

In recognition of the rapid fall of steam, the British Transport Commission decided to save a number of locomotives, carriages and wagons for posterity in order to tell the story of Britain's railways to future generations. It had to strike a balance between telling the story of Britain's railways, saving historically significant designs, and ensuring that there would be somewhere to keep what it had saved. Bear in mind that the only preserved railways at this time were the narrow-gauge Talyllyn and Ffestiniog Railways (totally unusable for storage of standard-gauge equipment); the standard-gauge Middleton Railway near Leeds, and the extremely embryonic Bluebell Railway near Horsted Keynes.

Inevitably, there were tough decisions. The LMS lost its Patriots, Royal Scots, and Princesses, the Great Western missed out on its Halls, Manors, Granges and Moguls. British Railways was well-represented, as was the Southern, but for the LNER, there were some huge gaps. A place in posterity was assured for the record-breaker, 4468 *Mallard*, and for the pioneering V2, *Green Arrow*, but there was no room for the ultimate expression of LNER locomotive design – the Peppercorn-designed A1 – nor for Gresley's freight designs, nor one of Thompson's go-anywhere B1s. But the most glaring omission, the most inexcusable, was

that none of Gresley's first Pacifics – the first, and arguably
the most successful Pacifics in Britain – was on the list for
preservation. It was a scandal. The reason given at the time
was that only one locomotive of a given wheel-arrangement
per designer could be preserved – patent nonsense, given
that both *Caerphilly Castle* and *King George V* of the Great
Western (both 4-6-0s) had been listed for preservation, as
well as two Southern Railway 4-6-0s.

The commission, it seems, looked at preserving *Great
Northern* but, because of Thompson's alterations, rejected
her on the grounds of suitability and cost of conversion.
They may also have felt that, as an A3 wasn't the original
design Gresley had penned in 1922, the type was unsuitable
anyway, but that's a specious argument. Two A3s could each
have justified a place on the list: the 108mph *Papyrus* and,
more important still, the record-breaking *Flying Scotsman*,
the most viewed, and probably the most loved of all. They
were denied it because the BTC felt that Gresley's big
designs were suitably represented by *Mallard* and *Green
Arrow*.

Enthusiasts around the country were outraged and
sought to persuade the Commission to change its mind.
There was a precedent for this when the flamboyant
secretary of the Gainsborough Model Railway Society,
George Hinchcliffe, led a massive letter-writing campaign
that persuaded the Commission to save one of the old Great
Central's delightful 'Director' class (so called because they
were named after directors of the company), *Butler-
Henderson*. Pegler, thanks to his place on the Eastern area

board, had also lobbied hard to preserve *Butler-Henderson* in the 1950s, and had ultimately been successful. Since then, Pegler had been keeping a watchful eye on the British Transport Commission's list, and had asked the Eastern Region's general manager to let him know if anything was heard about *Flying Scotsman*'s future.

When the list was published in 1961, Pegler, like many others, was aghast: 'The situation was intolerable. I was horrified at the prospect of seeing this marvellous class wiped out, and I resolved that if the State wouldn't correct this injustice, then I jolly well would!' Others felt the same, and in Scotland a group of railway enthusiasts led by Ramsey Ferguson decided to form a society to preserve an A3. They started raising money, and, thanks to publicity in railway magazines of the time, donations started to come in. In October 1962 they revealed that they wanted to preserve *Flying Scotsman* and started the first 'Save Our Scotsman' appeal; within eight weeks more than 300 people had joined, and almost £1,000 had been raised – not bad at a time when £10 a week was considered a good wage. The group was nothing if not ambitious (it would be like trying to buy a Jumbo jet from British Airways today), for it was an astonishing notion that a private group of individuals could buy something as massive and complicated as a steam locomotive. It must have been hard at times to prove they were serious – but they needed to, because time was running out.

Just weeks later British Railways announced that the pioneer A4 Pacific, *Silver Link*, was destined for the cutter's torch, and then, in December, Pegler received a letter from the Eastern Region. It was bad news. *Flying Scotsman* was going to be withdrawn for scrap in January. She was available for purchase before then, but she would cost the whopping sum of £3,000, and the A3 society had only raised £1,000. Pegler felt he had to act, and within forty-eight hours of receiving the letter, he hot-footed it to Scotland to meet Ferguson. He asked straight: 'Can you raise the extra £2,000?' Ferguson was equally honest in return. 'No,' he said. For a second, time stood still as Pegler weighed, for the last time, the decision he was about to make. Should he take the plunge and spend a huge amount on a steam locomotive he didn't need, had nowhere to keep, and little chance of running – or should he keep his wallet closed and trust to providence that somebody else would save this icon?

He'd probably made his mind up soon after receiving the letter from the Eastern Region, but his heart must have been beating a tattoo as he told Ferguson, as calmly as he could, that he was going to try to buy *Flying Scotsman* – and, not only that, was going to attempt to keep her running on the main line. For his part, Ferguson must have had mixed feelings: delight that the locomotive might be saved, and sadness that his group's bold and daring bid to secure her was now out of the running. Ferguson would later be instrumental in setting up the Gresley Society and preserving some of the engineer's lesser-known designs.

So *Flying Scotsman* had side-stepped the scrapman at the very last minute. Pegler returned from Scotland and swiftly sealed the sale. There were to be no discounts on the £3,000 asking price, even to an area board member, but he resolved to get some extras thrown in as part of the purchase price.

With express passenger steam on the old LNER main line rapidly fading away with the entry into traffic of the 3,000-horsepower 'Deltic' diesels, there must have been mixed feelings in the corridors of power of the Eastern Region about this swift and brutal transfer. Progress was one thing, but traditions built up over decades were being swept away. Somebody must have felt inclined to make a gesture in favour of steam, because the sale of *Flying Scotsman* was handled directly by the Eastern Region and not by British Railways' Central Supplies department, which handled all sales after that. In return for his £3,000, Pegler got *Flying Scotsman* herself, and, just as crucially, she was given a complete overhaul, converted back to single-chimney form and repainted into the colour that suited her best: LNER apple-green. He even got two main-line test runs from Doncaster to Peterborough and back thrown in. Added together, the extras can't have been worth much less than the locomotive: it was a great deal.

Ferguson had kept the Save Our Scotsman fund running in case Pegler wasn't successful, or changed his mind, and efforts were still being made to raise money. Pegler was president of the Gainsborough Model Railway Society, one of the most respected institutions of its type in the country then, and it was at its annual dinner that the first mention of the impending purchase was made. Pegler was passed a plate for donations to the Save Our Scotsman campaign but, to the shock of the members, he politely declined to contribute. Surely, they must have wondered, their president (and a very wealthy man to boot) couldn't possibly refuse to support such a worthy cause, could he?

Pegler, conscious of the reaction, leaned over to the Society's secretary, George Hinchcliffe, and whispered *sotto voce*: 'Sorry about that, but the reason I didn't donate was that I've just bought the whole blooming engine!' After a few seconds absorbing the shock, Hinchcliffe recovered and the dinner continued unabated.

Chapter Nine
Indian Summer

hough Pegler understandably wanted to keep it quiet, the deal was too good to stay a secret for long, and within weeks this rich businessman from Retford became national news: the first person to buy such a big locomotive in Britain. And he was only just in time, because *Flying Scotsman*'s last revenue-earning train for British Railways was to be the 1315 King's Cross to Leeds on 14 January 1963.

When it came, 14 January was a cold, crisp winter's day with snow on the ground across much of the country. The skies were largely clear, with some high clouds, and the sun was bright. It was a day tailor-made for watching steam trains, and it was a perfect day for marking the impending end of an era. The event might have been something of a wake, yet, thanks to Pegler, it became a celebration. The public's imagination had been fired by this former pilot indulging his passion for steam. There were journalists, newsreel cameras and photographers everywhere, even film cameras from as far away as the United States and Canada: King's Cross has probably never been so busy.

Pegler, inevitably, was at the centre of things. He spent two bitterly freezing hours at Top Shed, where, in footplate crew overalls, he did interview after interview. Eventually the moment came for *Flying Scotsman* to leave Top Shed for the last time in public ownership and reverse on to her train. Everywhere that there was a vantage point, crowds amassed to say *au revoir*. The Station Master had his top hat on, people thronged the tracks: it was like a royal occasion. Perhaps, in a sense, it was.

As departure time approached, Pegler stood on the footplate with a red carnation in his hand and signed autographs. 'It was the proudest day of my life,' he says. On the stroke of a quarter past one the guard blew his whistle, and, with a hiss of steam from the cylinder draincocks and just the faintest hint of a slip, *Flying Scotsman* took her final public train north.

From the footbridges of Finsbury Park to the platforms of Potters Bar and the streets of Stevenage, thousands of well-wishers braved the cold to mark the grand finale of East Coast Main Line steam. (It wasn't the last steam-hauled train from King's Cross, true, but it was the last hurrah, and the public wanted to mark it.)

A newsreel crew accompanied the train, and their film shows that the crowds really had to be seen to be believed. At Peterborough, their cheers can clearly be heard on the sound track, and the station was absolutely packed. After the stop at Peterborough *Flying Scotsman* dug her heels in and gritted her teeth in preparation for the climb up Stoke Bank – the same hill where *Mallard* had beaten the Germans so many years before – and then on towards Retford, which she passed four minutes early.

Then, at the level crossing at the now-closed Barnby Moor & Sutton station, the site of Pegler's earliest railway memories, Pegler hung on the whistle chain for what seemed like minutes in noisy acknowledgement of his family and friends, who had gathered for a rather chilly and unseasonal picnic. It was proving to be an epic run, but it had to come to an end, and as she slowed for the approaches to Doncaster the enormity of what he had done must have hit Pegler: he had saved an icon that had irrefutably demonstrated how loved it really was. She arrived at Doncaster six minutes early, and was uncoupled from the train, to be replaced by another locomotive. She then went more or less straight into the works where she was built for overhaul.

Doncaster Works showed just what they could do, giving *Flying Scotsman* a complete overhaul in just twenty-four days, and at the end of February 1963, now restored to her original single-chimney form, she undertook two trial runs from Doncaster to Peterborough and back. She hadn't yet been repainted, and she looked somewhat forlorn, but mechanically speaking she was now in mint condition and raring to go. Pegler, who was on the footplate on both runs, looked the part of her proud owner, brimming with confidence and pride.

She finally emerged from Doncaster works, like a butterfly from a chrysalis, on 26 March 1963, and it was clear her links with British Railways were severed. The dull Brunswick green paint had been replaced by sparkling apple green, and she had acquired a corridor tender from one of the remaining streamlined A4s. She was absolutely immaculate, and Pegler must have felt, for a moment at least, that it would be a crying shame to run her and spoil the craftsman's finish on her!

Pegler's plan was to run *Flying Scotsman* on charter trains across the network, but to do that he needed to get a deal with British Railways. His solicitor drew up heads of agreement with the chief solicitor of the British Railways Board, and while it didn't immediately allow Pegler to do anything at all, it did provide the contractual process to make it happen. One of its provisos was that Pegler could run *Flying Scotsman* on British Railways until 1966, with options that could take it up to 1971. This was crucial for Pegler, because at the time, there was simply nowhere else he could run her! He had also agreed to lease a former locomotive weigh-house at the end of Platform 8 at Doncaster for £65 per year. All this was handled by the Deputy Chairman of the British Railways Board, Sir Stuart Mitchell. Mitchell was supportive of *Flying Scotsman* – 'he thought it would be rather fun,' recalls Pegler – and put the plans in motion, neglecting, whether by accident or design, to tell his boss. His boss, the chairman of the British Railways Board, was a balding man with a toothbrush moustache called Dr Beeching.

In 1963, despite the Modernisation Plan, British Railways was in crisis and losing money hand over fist. A deficit of £65.9 million in 1961 became a deficit of £82 million in 1962. Business – particularly freight – was being lost to roads, and the economies that were supposed to be brought by replacing steam with diesel traction simply weren't making the slightest difference. Time, then, for some radical thinking.

Beeching, previously a director of ICI, had been

appointed as somebody from outside the railways to knock them into shape. He would apply the principles of business to the railway, and all would then be well and good. In a report called 'The Reshaping of British Railways' Beeching's team pointed out that eighty per cent of the traffic generated by the railways was carried on just a fifth of the network. He proposed that many of the duplicated routes should close, and that other lines should lose their passenger services to concentrate on freight alone. Of Britain's 18,000 miles of railways, Beeching wanted to close 6,000. Furthermore, he argued that many services could be more cheaply provided by buses. It wasn't all cuts though: he also recommended extensive electrification and the introduction of more efficient methods of operation. Beeching gets the blame for what followed, but in truth, that's a case of shooting the messenger. It was the politicians, once again meddling where they had no knowledge, who started to disassemble a sustainable transport system that had been built over the course of 150 years, with no thought that it might be needed in the future.

The cuts proposed by Beeching centred on revenues, but not always fairly. A main station in a town might generate a great deal of revenue from ticket sales, while a seaside resort station, by virtue of the fact that most passengers would be arriving from elsewhere, would generate little revenue itself, even though its existence was making money for other stations on the network. The approach was thus fatally flawed, but that didn't bother the politicians and civil servants.

The big problem was that too many revenue centres were deprived of their markets, and that business simply stayed away from rail. Passengers hated the bus replacement services, while many freight customers simply had little choice other than to abandon rail. The effects compounded themselves, and as the branches were pruned, so the whole tree suffered. Of course, there were those who suggest that, when losses were running at £100 million, saving £7 million by cutting a third of the network was worth doing – but communities crying out for rail services would surely disagree today. Ironically, though, the carnage wreaked on the rail network in the 1960s ultimately benefited *Flying Scotsman*, because it paved the way for the railway preservation movement to flourish.

Perhaps Pegler's most outstanding achievement, however, was not buying *Flying Scotsman*, or even the extras on the deal: it was the extraordinary deal he struck with British Railways to run *Flying Scotsman* on the main line. Beeching was furious at this. He found out about Mitchell's agreement with Pegler for the weigh-house at Doncaster and, in Pegler's words, hit the roof: 'He'd obviously not read the newspapers properly in January!' Beeching saw Pegler as a dangerous maverick who could tarnish the image of British Railways and must be stopped. The railways were undergoing a painful process of modernisation, and in the early 1960s – when all the talk was of the space race, the Cold War, the white heat of technology – the steam railway looked very, very old. Running *Flying Scotsman* on the network, Beeching argued, would send out entirely the wrong message about Britain's railways, and should not be allowed, so he immediately forbade Pegler to run *Flying Scotsman* on the main line. Pegler countered with the contract signed with the BRB's chief solicitor, and Beeching, outwitted, issued a stern directive banning future deals similar to *Flying Scotsman*'s from being signed.

It seems that Beeching was also upset that it was an area board member who had signed this deal. He decided to fire Pegler because running a steam locomotive was detrimental to the railway: the exact reverse of Sir Brian Robertson's reason for appointing him. Pegler asked for a head-to-head meeting with Beeching.

'I'd just like to know for my own satisfaction,' Pegler asked him, 'is the reason I'm being dropped from the area board anything to do with the fact that I bought *Flying Scotsman*?'

Beeching sat back in his chair and looked Pegler straight in the eye. After a pause that must have felt, even to Pegler, like a thousand years, he responded:

'Well, as a matter of fact, yes.'

'Thanks very much,' said Pegler. 'That's all I wanted to know.'

Pegler, still an extremely wealthy man, wasn't fazed by this official disapproval, and swiftly moved to ensure that *Flying Scotsman* got the tender loving care she deserved. To look after her, he hired the retired Doncaster driver Edgar Hoyle, who on an epic run with A4 4498 *Sir Nigel Gresley* in the 1950s was running well at 112mph and looking in good form to beat *Mallard* when the locomotive inspector eased the regulator. To help run the tours he had in mind for *Flying Scotsman* he also brought in George Hinchcliffe, a school teacher in Gainsborough, who in his spare time was Secretary of the Gainsborough Model Railway Society. Hinchcliffe had worked with Pegler for years, first helping to market rail tours in the 1950s, and from 1963 promoting *Flying Scotsman* too. He was an enthusiast almost from birth, and as he grew up he proved an expert blagger of footplate rides and a naturally brilliant fireman. War service interrupted his engineering apprenticeship, and when he returned from the Navy he became a teacher instead. Without Hinchcliffe, Pegler and *Flying Scotsman* would not have been nearly as successful, and Pegler's decision to appoint him was nothing short of inspired.

Everything was now in place, and in honour of the Ffestiniog Railway, Pegler planned the first train in private ownership to take enthusiasts from London Paddington to Wales to see Pegler's spectacular narrow-gauge line.

On the morning of 20 April 1963, *Flying Scotsman* backed on to her train in Brunel's cathedral to steam at Paddington. She was probably the first ex-LNER Pacific locomotive to visit the station since 60033 *Seagull* in the 1948 locomotive exchanges, and she was almost certainly the first of Gresley's initial design of Pacific to visit since A1 No. 4474 *Victor Wild* back in 1925. To the local enthusiasts, by then more used to diesels than steam, *Flying Scotsman* was a poignant reminder of past glories, and they came in their droves to witness this unusual and stirring sight.

As she headed north, it was clear that the public's enthusiasm for the old lady had, if anything, grown since her last run in BR service. Though undoubtedly helped by the fact that an A3 was a complete stranger to these lines, crowds flocked to every vantage point they could to see her. At Birmingham's much-missed old Snow Hill station, 8,000 fans (a football crowd, according to one commentator) jammed the platforms, footbridges and even the tracks to get a glimpse – and Snow Hill was a pretty big station then. Such were the numbers that the police had to be called in to keep order. And so it went on, up through Shrewsbury, on the old Great Western's main line to Chester, as far as Ruabon, where *Flying Scotsman* had to give way to a smaller locomotive because of weight and size restrictions on the line through mid-Wales. It was the first time this queen of locomotives had visited the Principality. If Pegler had had any doubts in his mind whatsoever about the appeal of *Flying Scotsman*, they were well-and-truly blown away by the end of the journey.

In May the second tour ran, this time for the Gainsborough Model Railway Society, which had supported Pegler so steadfastly. It ran from Lincoln to Southampton – more new territory for *Flying Scotsman* – and the scenes from the first run were repeated. Everyone wanted to get a glimpse of *Flying Scotsman*, it seemed.

And now came the point when Hinchcliffe's long experience of helping Pegler run the rail tours in the 1950s really paid off. Not all the runs were ten-coach epics. *Flying Scotsman* made her next appearance back in London in

October 1963, not at the head of a massive, named express but hauling a two-coach special for members of the Bassetlaw Conservative Association on a visit to the capital. Pegler, as ever, was on the footplate, though stringent – and reasonable – restrictions imposed by British Railways meant that only an experienced and qualified driver could take the regulator. Pegler was in his element on the tours, playing the part of showman to perfection. He would go through the train talking to passengers, signing books, and adored seeing smiling, happy children on them. Charities also benefited, particularly in one spectacular run a couple of years later.

The tours continued, and in 1964 *Flying Scotsman* visited her namesake country for the first time in twenty-five years. Pegler chartered the prestigious 'Master Cutler' carriages to run a special 'Pegler's Pullman' train from Doncaster to Edinburgh Waverley, a run well within the locomotive's capabilities. She wasn't the only steam locomotive on the old East Coast Main Line on 9 May 1964, but she was one of an ever-shrinking handful: the last few Gresley Pacifics were going out in a last blaze of glory on the difficult and strenuous line from Edinburgh to Aberdeen.

Pegler had wanted a painting of *Flying Scotsman* for a long time, and he commissioned one of the greatest railway artists ever, Terence Cuneo (a statue of whom sits proudly on the concourse of London Waterloo), to paint a picture of the locomotive on the most iconic railway structure of all, the Forth Bridge. The problem, though, was that an artist naturally needs a sitting, but parking *Flying Scotsman* on the Forth Bridge while Cuneo worked his magic on canvas was likely to cause one or two problems. Pegler persevered. He approached his old friend Willie Thorpe, by then the boss of the Scottish Region and cheekily asked Thorpe whether he could 'borrow' the Forth Bridge for two or three days while Cuneo painted *Flying Scotsman*. Thorpe, surely with a twinkle in his eye, said 'Oh yes, we can arrange that.'

'And it caused absolute chaos,' explained Pegler later. 'It was sort of sat on the Forth Bridge for about three days and had to get out of the way of the fish train from Aberdeen, which in those days was still running, and various other things. But it was an absolutely extraordinary experience!'

Only Pegler could possibly have pulled off such an extraordinary stunt, and the result is one of the greatest railway paintings ever: Cuneo captured *Flying Scotsman* to perfection, racing underneath the first of the great cantilevers, a wisp of steam at the safety valves, and more from the injectors – poetry in motion captured in still-life.

By the end of 1964, *Flying Scotsman* had covered enough miles to need an intermediate overhaul, but her birthplace at Doncaster was no longer able to perform the necessary work. She would have to go north, to the old North Eastern Railway works at Darlington. Here, continuing the proud North Eastern tradition, she had her cylinder casings painted green, something that had never been done before on a Gresley Pacific. It was a sign of affection from the staff: the hatchet between the old GNR and NER had finally been buried.

The start of 1965 really marked the beginning of the end of the steam railway. Most of the grand old classes – the

Great Western's Kings and Castles, the Duchesses and Princesses of the LMS, the LNER Pacifics, had all gone, or were well on their way out. Only the Southern Region, which had arguably the most modern-designed express steam locomotives and wanted to keep them until electrification of key routes was complete, really supported steam. Most of the steam locomotives left were either heavy freight locomotives (invariably the LMS 8F or BR 9F types) or mixed-traffic locomotives along the lines of Thompson's B1. This made *Flying Scotsman* more precious than ever, because now, with one or two exceptions, wherever she went she would be the only express steam passenger locomotive around. She was also, though, a massive contrast with the increasingly filthy, ever more work-stained survivors of steam in BR service. Unlike them, she was immaculate.

Many years before, the Great Western Railway ran a Cheltenham to London express with the highest average speed of any train in the world at the time, around 71 mph. The train was invariably hauled by a Castle, and the Western Region remained proud of its past glories. However, since the record had been set, Gresley's Pacifics had been transformed by better boilers, valves and draughting. Pegler reckoned, with good reason, that on a similar five-coach train, *Flying Scotsman* ought to be able to smash the GWR's long-standing record, even within the 80mph speed limit imposed on the engine by BR.

A tour organised by the *The Railway Magazine* on 9 October 1965 from Paddington to the Welsh Valleys provided the opportunity, and in anticipation of an epoch-making run, a

TV crew hired a plane to film *Flying Scotsman*. The journey started well, with a clear run; the 36 miles to Reading was done in just thirty-two minutes – not much slower than the twenty-five-or-so minutes diesel trains take today – and it looked like the record attempt was most definitely on. *Flying Scotsman* was absolutely flying along the Great Western Main Line, motion blurring with the speed, and the chimney simmering with exhaust. As she approached Swindon, the atmosphere on the train started to bubble as the passengers started to realise just how well they were running. But it was too good to last: *Flying Scotsman*'s front end was suddenly wreathed in steam, and the crew had no option other than to shut off steam and coast into the station. *Flying Scotsman* had committed the cardinal sin of failing on the road – a rare occurrence for the A3s at any time. 'If an engine could blush,' said Pegler, '*Scotsman* would have been doing so.'

On shed, it became clear that eight bolts on the back left-hand steam chest had worked loose. It was the work of a saboteur, presumably hell-bent on ensuring that the Great Western retained its record. Some railway enthusiasts have particular loyalties, either to companies, or to types of locomotive, and many a lively debate as to their merits or otherwise has taken place, but this was going too far. Pegler's insurance company confirmed the suspicions: the bolts 'had been deliberately slacked off with malicious intent', read its report. Loyalty to a company is one thing, but whoever did this put a national icon at risk, and if the crew hadn't shut off when they did, potentially put passengers in danger.

Pegler was undeterred, and a month later ran a luxury Pullman train from Paddington to Cardiff in aid of the World Wildlife Fund. *Flying Scotsman* carried a jaunty headboard, and the train was colloquially known as 'The Panda Express'. A security guard was placed on her to deter a repeat sabotage attempt, and this time, *Flying Scotsman* was free to run without interruption. Driven by ex-Great Western driver Williams and Fireman Wallis, she reached Swindon in 65 minutes 26 seconds: ten minutes faster than the Great Western's schedule, though the overall record of just less than fifty-seven minutes, set in 1932, remained with the GWR. *Flying Scotsman* reached Cardiff in 2 hours 17 minutes, and it's widely reckoned that neither the GWR nor British Railways was ever able to achieve this with steam.

Throughout 1965 *Flying Scotsman* kept people's attention. Crowd after crowd thronged the lineside for a glimpse. Dozens of schools booked trips behind her, and the Prime Minister, Harold Wilson even got a cab-ride in the locomotive. By the end of the year, she had more than recouped the £3,000 Pegler paid for her in 1963: not a bad return for an old girl.

But, as 1965 turned to 1966, it was becoming increasingly apparent that depending on continued supplies of coal and water from British Railways was becoming increasingly precarious. Rapid dieselisation meant that many water towers were being removed, as were the water troughs which enabled a steam locomotive to refresh its tender on the move. To ensure continued operation, Pegler established a separate company called *Flying Scotsman* Enterprises, and placed the charismatic George Hinchcliffe in charge. To Hinchcliffe fell the task of securing coal and water supplies, and of negotiating with BR to get precious timetable slots – BR had taken the reasonable enough decision that *Flying Scotsman* could only run at a given time if she didn't interfere with scheduled services used by ordinary passengers.

Dealing with BR proved a particular challenge for Hinchcliffe, who recalled in his memoirs:

> I was fortunate to deal with only two BR officers throughout the period when I ran *Flying Scotsman*, first for Pegler, and later for Bill McAlpine.
>
> Working with BR was an art-form in itself. It was almost impossible to make a frontal approach whenever a steam engine was involved. The reason was simple: the BR policy was totally against steam – yet those in authority with whom I did business had a sneaking respect for them, so there was a conflict, and it is a wonder to me how we ever turned a wheel!

Pegler concurs; dealing as a private individual with a giant nationalised company could be extremely difficult, yet there were those in BR who did their very best to help. The Chief Mechanical Engineer of the British Railways Board, Terry Miller, proved an absolute godsend, offering sound advice, and trying to find a way through the inevitable mass of red tape. This was just as well because as 1966 continued, getting enough water to *Flying Scotsman* was proving a real headache. A road tanker was invariably on-hand, but pumping it was slow in the extreme – and *Flying Scotsman* could carry something like 4,000 gallons of water without difficulty.

Miller was a far-sighted man, and when Darlington Works was about to close in 1966 he tipped Pegler off that he would need to be self-sufficient in future. He secured a spare boiler and cylinders for *Flying Scotsman*; they were from an A3, No. 60041 *Salmon Trout*, and were identical to *Flying Scotsman*'s fittings. With time running out for main-line steam, it was a simple case of acquiring them while he could, and Pegler immediately regarded it as a good acquisition.

Miller also suggested that Pegler could get another tender for *Flying Scotsman* to carry water, connected to her existing tender by a flexible hose. Pegler readily agreed, but stipulated: 'I want a corridor tender, so I can get through!' This would prove easier said than done, as in 1966 the streamlined A4 Pacifics which carried the last corridor tenders were finally withdrawn. Miller eventually found one, from No. 60009 *Union of South Africa* (a locomotive that would later, thankfully, be preserved), and converted it to carry just water. The tender cost £1,000, but converting it into a water carrier cost another £6,000 – double the purchase price of the locomotive it was to be hauled by! Nevertheless, it was money well spent, and it ensured that *Flying Scotsman* could run independently of BR's watering facilities.

Flying Scotsman eventually left its small shed at Doncaster station and moved to the town's main depot, Carr. This was extensively converted to diesel operation in 1966, but Pegler used his main-line agreement to persuade BR to keep one line open to maintain steam locomotives, complete with pits and the crucial watering and boiler washing-out facilities.

Beeching's insistence that no other operating deals like *Flying Scotsman*'s should be concluded meant that by 1967 she was the only privately owned locomotive allowed to run on British Railways. After Pegler bought *Flying Scotsman*, a number of wealthy individuals, led by Billy Butlin, had brought locomotives from British Railways, and some, including *Pendennis Castle*, and the Southern Region's *Clan Line* had been used on charter trains. No more! Steam was being eliminated with ruthless haste, and it was only grudging respect for the letter of Pegler's deal that kept *Flying Scotsman* running. So the tours continued throughout 1967, and, increasingly, *Flying Scotsman* was the only steam locomotive to be seen in many places. Equally, the number of places that she could go to had been steadily diminishing thanks to Beeching's axe (though by now it was Labour's transport secretary Barbara Castle who was doing most of the chopping).

Steam held out on the Southern Region until 1967 with Bulleid's rebuilt 'Merchant Navy' and 'Battle of Britain'/'West Country' Pacifics holding sway on express services alongside the last handful of the original air-smoothed Bulleid Pacifics. The BR Standards were also able to continue in service with the Southern Region until 1967. Electric trains had been introduced on the Southern Region as early as the 1920s, so it is ironic that it was one of the last to use steam traction on express services. But its policy was straightforward: it wanted to electrify its routes quickly, so why buy diesel trains which would soon be made redundant in any case? As with the other regions, steam was run down during its final years in Southern service, nameplates were removed, number plates disappeared, and a thick coat of grime penetrated every area of the locomotives. Somehow the Southern Pacifics continued to put in impressive performances, regularly reaching speeds of around 100mph on the main line from London to Basingstoke, but nothing could stop the irresistible progress of modernisation.

Chapter Ten
Non-stop Swan-song

As 1968 dawned the writing was on the wall. This would be the last year of British Railways' steam operation. Characteristically, Pegler wanted to ensure that it went out with a bang. For years, he'd dreamt of one last non-stop run between London and Edinburgh, and 1 May 1968 was the fortieth anniversary of *Flying Scotsman*'s epic run from King's Cross. Pegler badgered, harangued, pestered and pleaded with BR management for the chance to repeat that run, and on 28 February 1968 the Eastern Region's legendary boss, Gerard Fiennes, gave it the green light.

Perhaps it was this that proved the final nail in Fiennes' BR coffin, for he was unceremoniously dumped from office just five days after approving Pegler's ambitious scheme. A month later, to his dismay, but surely to little surprise, Pegler was told that *Flying Scotsman*'s last ever non-stop run was off. Frantic negotiations ensued, and, after Pegler offered to bring a £5,000 payment forward, the decision was reversed with just three weeks to go. There wasn't much time to prepare.

If Pegler had left it even a couple of years to try to repeat the epic run, he would have failed. Even with her second tender, there were doubts about whether *Flying Scotsman* could carry enough water to make it without the water troughs that had been used for decades to top up the tenders (via a scoop lowered into the troughs on the move). However, despite seemingly being made redundant by the new diesels, some water troughs were in fact still being used (to top up the steam heating boilers carried by diesels, to ensure that passengers stayed nice and warm). There were three sets still in use on the East Coast Man Line, and *Flying Scotsman* would need to make full use of all to stand a chance.

On 1 May 1968, for the last time, a Gresley Pacific stood at the head of its train at King's Cross waiting for the 10.00 departure time – next stop, Edinburgh. This was high-profile stuff, and the BBC put a film crew on board to record a documentary. Main-line steam had less than five months to live, and this was one of the last rites. Nobody wanted to miss it, and King's Cross was once again crowded with onlookers eager to watch steam's final fling.

Pegler was brimming with excitement. Five years after he'd bought *Flying Scotsman*, he looked much the same. He was still a tall, well-built man; the hair was a little thinner, but his moustache was as neatly trimmed as ever, and the fire was still burning in his eyes. Even Pegler was on tenterhooks however: 'I suppose it's like a diver on the high board – now this is happening, I can't wait to get on with it.' Conscious that his agreement with BR still had time to run, he also paid tribute to the nationalised railway:

The objective as far as I'm concerned was to have a go, and it's an extraordinary thing, in my opinion anyway, that on a great nationalised undertaking, one can take out a privately owned piece of machinery forty-five years old and hitch it up to a train of BR stock and take 300 people almost 400 miles on a weekday amid all the other services.

Let's face it, this is a pretty sporting gesture by the British Railways Board.

Exactly on time, she pulled away gently from King's Cross, a 'Deltic'-hauled express keeping pace. Gathering speed, she entered the leftmost portal of Gasworks Tunnel, the sound of the diesel clearly audible through the walls. Emerging into daylight just ahead of the 'Deltic', she got her head down and started charging, but imperiously the 'Deltic' overhauled the veteran steam locomotive. It was rather as if the baton had finally, formally and irretrievably, been passed from steam to diesel.

The passengers on the train were a mixed bunch, from lucky young train-spotters, eagerly taking down all the numbers they possibly could, to Captain Holmes and his wife, who were celebrating the fortieth anniversary of the day they met. On 1 May 1928 they had shared a compartment on the very first non-stop run and, in the words of the husband, got on like a house on fire. The wife was initially disappointed to find that there was also a parson in the compartment, but she changed her mind about him when he offered to escort the pair for lunch, allowing them to stay together while still presenting a respectable appearance: in 1928, such things still mattered. They were engaged within three weeks, and were still very much in love forty years on.

Also on the train was the Reverend Wilbert Awdry, who by 1968 was hugely respected as the author of the Thomas the Tank Engine stories. Like many men of the cloth, Awdry found himself attracted to the railways, and wanted to mark the occasion in the best way possible. Explaining the appeal of steam, he said simply: 'It's the smell of smoke and the beat of the engine – and the feeling of being pulled not by a mechanical box on wheels, but by something pulsing and alive.'

Hinchcliffe had arranged for a road tanker to be available in case of emergency at Berwick-upon-Tweed, but nobody expected to need it. The first troughs, at Scrooby, were 130 miles from London, and though the water levels seemed low, enough was picked up for the moment. As the train approached Arksey, near Doncaster, disaster almost struck. A broken rail meant a danger signal for *Flying Scotsman*. Pegler, in the cab of *Flying Scotsman*, his sooty-black face glistening with a sheen of sweat, got twitchy, peering over the cab sidesheets to see if the signal had cleared. Crawling at less than walking pace, one of the crew jumped off the engine and ran to the nearest signal telephone to get permission to proceed. Just two seconds before *Flying Scotsman* would have had to stop, the signal turned to green, the crew member climbed up, and she was on her way again. Pegler breathed a sigh of relief: 'It was a damn sight too near for comfort,' he said.

It was like the glory days, when all the top-link express trains were that clean – unlike many of the last remaining passenger trains hauled by steam – and *Flying Scotsman* didn't

Flying Scotsman appeals to all ages. Is it the size, the smell, the sound – or just that gorgeous green colour – entrancing six-year-old Hannah Styles? *Press Association*

Hornby's train sets have kept *Flying Scotsman* in the public eye for decades, and are still immensely popular – as well as the only way most enthusiasts will ever get to drive her! *Reproduced by permission of Hornby*

Sir Nigel Gresley, the locomotive's designer (left, in bowler hat), hoped the advanced 'Hush Hush' No. 10000 would supersede *Flying Scotsman* and her ilk. She proved an expensive failure and forced him to develop *Flying Scotsman*'s design into its ultimate form, the streamlined 'A4'.
National Railway Museum

Flying Scotsman owes much to the very successful 'K4' Pacifics, built by the Pennsylvania Railroad in the USA. Though far too big for use in Britain, the 'K4''s proportions were used by Gresley in *Flying Scotsman*. *Colour-Rail*

Flying Scotsman was wrapped in protective cladding when she was towed to the Empire Exhibition at Wembley in 1924 – nothing was allowed to damage her glowing paintwork. *National Railway Museum*

It was this arresting sight of *Flying Scotsman*, the star attraction at the Empire Exhibition, that so captivated Alan Pegler, then aged four, that he ultimately bought the locomotive. *Corbis*

Driver Bill Sparshatt and Fireman Webster greet the crowds at King's Cross after *Flying Scotsman*'s record-breaking 100mph run in 1934. Their status as elite railwaymen is clear. *National Railway Museum*

Flying Scotsman in BR days when allocated to Leicester Central. *Milepost 92½*

Flying Scotsman at King's Cross servicing point where locomotives were stabled between duties, in 1962. The English Electric Type 4 diesel on the right was no more powerful – but presaged the imminent extinction of the steam railway. *Getty Images*

Alan Pegler stands next to *Flying Scotsman* on 14 January 1963. By the end of her journey to Doncaster, he would have finally saved her for the nation. *Press Association*

On 20 April 1963, *Flying Scotsman* hauled her first rail tour under Pegler's custodianship, from Paddington to Wales. By this time, steam was in full retreat on the old Great Western lines. *Colour-Rail*

Accompanying *Flying Scotsman* to the USA was a bevy of beauties to sell souvenirs. Though popular, they were always overshadowed by the 'old lady' they supported! *Press Association*

Flying Scotsman in Boston during her tour of the USA, complete with formidable cowcatcher, headlight and bell. *Brian Sharpe, Mortons Media*

In April 2006 at King's Cross Sir William McAlpine, *Flying Scotsman*'s subsequent owner, is awarded the accolade of a locomotive named after him. *Justin Perkins*

Flying Scotsman running near Wagga Wagga in Australia on its way from Sydney to Melbourne in Australia, October 1988. *Brian Sharpe, Mortons Media*

When *Flying Scotsman* pulled into Alice Springs in August 1989 after an epic 30-hour, 775-mile journey from Broken Hill, members of the Aboriginal community there mounted a ceremony to welcome the venerable engine to their territory in Central Australia. *courtesy of Roland Kennington*

The Sellafield Sightseer trains were a regular operation in the 1980s, but protests about the nuclear power station eventually forced their demise. Even so, this was typical of *Flying Scotsman*'s main line work in the 1980s. *Corbis / Milepost 92 1/2*

Dr Tony Marchington spent a fortune restoring *Flying Scotsman* at Southall in west London. Though his business plan would eventually fail, the restoration was one of the finest ever undertaken.
Press Association

On 9 July 2003, *Flying Scotsman*, hauling the Orient Express, passes another steam tour at Basingstoke, as well as a modern Southwest Trains commuter train, to mark the anniversary of the end of steam in the south of England.
Press Association

The people's engine: *Flying Scotsman* makes her debut in public ownership at York's Railfest in 2004. She received a rapturous reception, complete with bagpipes!
Press Association

Flying Scotsman hauled a series of popular trains from York to Scarborough in her first two years of NRM ownership. Here, she pulls away from Scarborough's classic signal gantry on her way home. *National Railway Museum*

Maintaining steam locomotives is hard work: apprentice engineer David Wright takes a well-earned break in *Flying Scotsman*'s smokebox during servicing at York. *Press Association*

Royal Ascot was held at York racecourse in 2005, and what better way to promote the city's most famous icon than with a suitable hat, worn by Sarah Mahmood. *Corbis*

disappoint. At Wiske Moor, she again picked up water and continued north. On the approach to Berwick the two locomotive inspectors, whose job it was to ensure the safe operation of the train, were becoming concerned about water levels. With two of the water pick-ups only regarded as average, there was a real possibility that *Flying Scotsman* might run out of water. They held a hurried conference on the footplate, and Pegler, not wanting to influence them, repaired to the buffet car. Still covered in grime, the tension on his face was clear, and his brow was furrowed: 'This is the highly dodgy situation I'd hoped we were not going to find ourselves in.' Pegler guessed that there were between 2,500 and 3,000 gallons in the tenders (a remarkably accurate assessment), and that they would make it without having to stop at Berwick for water. (His mood lightened when somebody pointed out that there were 1,800 bottles of beer on the train: 'I think the old girl would steam very well on light ale!' he beamed.) The decision wasn't his, however: it was down to Chief Locomotive Inspector Les Richards and his deputy George Harland. After their conference, Harland confirmed the good news: 'Inspector Richards and myself consider that with 3,000 gallons of water, we have sufficient to take us to Edinburgh.'

Had *Flying Scotsman* in fact been running low on water, the prearranged plan was for the engine crew to blow their whistle at Lucker, near Berwick, so that the Berwick signal-man, who would be listening for it, could prepare for their arrival. In the event, as she approached Lucker and its vital troughs, the driver spotted a photographer lying on his stomach on the edge of the platform trying to get the definitive shot of the day. There was no option: the driver hung on the whistle to encourage the photographer to get out of the way as the locomotive screamed through the station. Berwick's signalman heard the blast and prepared for the worst, setting the points so that *Flying Scotsman* could go into the goods loop for refreshment. It took much whistling and fist-shaking before *Flying Scotsman*'s frantic crew got their countermanding message through to the signalman, and the line was cleared for progress to continue at the last minute.

Flying Scotsman arrived in Edinburgh to a rapturous reception and the sound of bagpipes thirty minutes ahead of the 1928 schedule of 8 hours 15 minutes. Against the bureaucracy of British Rail, against the determined efforts of a photographer, and against all probability of it ever happening again, she had done it, and repeated history.

Pegler was congratulated by the Mayor of Edinburgh, and on the platforms a crowd ranging from elderly enthusiasts to mothers with young children cheered her arrival. Pegler summed up his feelings: 'I'm very delighted to have done it non-stop,' he said with understated pride – though he must have been bursting with excitement: *Flying Scotsman*'s run was a remarkable effort.

As soon as she arrived, Pegler climbed on to the tenders. The rear tender was empty. He moved forward to the front tender, and it was almost empty: the only water *Flying Scotsman* had left was in her boiler. It was that close. Appropriately, Nigel Gresley's beloved daughter Vi was on the train, and afterwards she said: 'I'm so proud. I only wish my father had been here to witness it.' Surely the great man would have been delighted to see his most adored creation prove what she could do one last time.

Three days later, a return non-stop run was attempted, and this time, concerned that the levels in the water troughs were low, one of *Flying Scotsman*'s supporters, Terry Robinson, obtained a set of keys to Scrooby troughs and held down the ball-cock to ensure they were full. This time there were no problems, and *Flying Scotsman* was greeted in King's Cross by thousands. But now it really was the end of an era. Hereafter nothing would ever be the same again.

Chapter Eleven

American Adventure

One of Pegler's long-held dreams was to show *Flying Scotsman* off to the world by taking her abroad, and particularly to the United States. There had been a long tradition of British locomotives flying the flag across the Atlantic, since the days of the London & North Western Railways' compound *Queen Empress* in 1893. In 1927 the Great Western's flagship *King George V* visited to celebrate the centenary of the Baltimore & Ohio Railroad; the LMS' *Royal Scot* was sent over for the 'Century of Progress' exposition in Chicago in 1933, and followed a few years later by the streamlined *Duchess of Hamilton* (disguised as the first-of-type *Coronation*), which because of the war, remained in the USA rather longer than planned, from 1939 to 1942. Pegler had a desperate yearning to take an LNER locomotive over the Atlantic – but the opportunity to do so seemed distant.

However, in 1965 the boss of Vermont's Steamtown preservation centre, a wonderful man called F Nelson Blount, met Pegler. The former dive-bomber pilot who owned *Flying Scotsman* and the charismatic, almost evangelical American hit it off immediately. Blount matched Pegler's enthusiasm inch for inch, and when Pegler floated the idea of an American tour, surely over a few drinks,

Blount offered to sponsor it. Pegler was flabbergasted, but Blount was serious, and soon Pegler was off to the United States to see if such a trip might be feasible at some point in the future.

It was early days, and *Flying Scotsman* still had plenty of work on rail tours in Britain to keep her busy. Nonetheless, ideas were firmed up, and gradually the idea of using *Flying Scotsman* to lead a trade mission took shape. It was certainly creative thinking, and from 1965 plans slowly developed. Thanks to Blount's generosity, it appeared that a tour would be feasible, both from a technical point of view and, crucially, from a financial one also. With the main-line agreement with BR due to expire in 1971, it seemed that after that might be a good time. Pegler's plans, however, were shattered when Blount died in a crash involving his private aeroplane. The sponsor was gone, and the dream was in ashes.

However, Pegler's devil-may-care enthusiasm carried him on. 'Having lost my sponsor,' he said, 'the sensible thing to do would have been to call it off, but by that time I'd become so fired with enthusiasm at the idea of touring America in my own train that I decided to go ahead anyway!' So he formed a new company, *Flying Scotsman* (USA) Ltd, and began to formulate plans. He was given a helping hand by the vice-president of the United States-based Southern Railway (nothing to do with Britain's Southern Railway), W Graham Claytor. The Southern Railway was celebrating its seventy-fifth anniversary in 1969, and Claytor offered to host the British locomotive, and to negotiate for the train to run on five other railways. With such goodwill, Pegler finally set his heart on *Flying Scotsman*'s greatest adventure yet.

One thing the train wouldn't be able to do was haul passengers, as American laws prevented that. *Flying Scotsman* would, however, be able to haul an exhibition or circus train. With the latter ruled out as being inappropriate and expensive (and there wasn't a spare circus available), Pegler opted to run an exhibition train. He had already been approached by a number of businessmen who wanted to showcase their products in the United States, and he thought *Flying Scotsman* would be a great ambassador for Britain, as she was likely to generate goodwill wherever she went. It was typical Pegler: bold and imaginative, and it didn't take long to persuade high-profile names such as Pretty Polly tights, British Petroleum, Lloyds Bank and the Royal Shakespeare Company to offer their backing for the venture. *Flying Scotsman* would be a brilliant gimmick to attract potential buyers to the exhibition, and the fact that it was on a self-contained train would mean that it could be seen by many more people than a static exhibition. It was good thinking, and at the time of 'Buy British', perfectly timed.

It was timed well for the government too, which had decided to present two Pullman carriages used by General Eisenhower and Winston Churchill during the war to the American National Railway Museum in Green Bay, Wisconsin. They could hitch a ride behind *Flying Scotsman*, and would be another popular attraction. Nor were they the only high-profile coaches in the train: an observation car was converted to resemble an English pub (providing a good promotional opportunity for another of the train's supporters, the brewer Watneys) and named 'The Fireman's Rest'. An administration coach was added to the train and five exhibition cars, a mixture of baggage and pigeon coaches Pegler had plucked from the scrap line at York for £200 each. These were painted in chocolate and cream colours to match the Pullmans, and had a Union Flag at one end, with a Stars & Stripes at the other to reflect the friendship between Britain and America.

The ever-present George Hinchcliffe was to manage the train, after arranging a sabbatical from his teaching job, while British Rail supplied, at Pegler's expense, drivers Norman Clark of Doncaster and Henry Fosters from Hornsey. Doncaster fireman David Court joined them, as did locomotive inspector Alan Richardson.

It was all coming together, and in anticipation of this, Pegler sent *Flying Scotsman* to the Leeds locomotive builders Hunslet for a major overhaul and replacement of her boiler tubes. These were major jobs now largely beyond the ability of BR works to undertake, as much of the vital equipment needed to overhaul steam locomotives had been disposed of, and those that had the ability lacked the capacity. At Hunslet, inspectors from the United States and Canada (which the tour was also to visit) transport authorities ran the rule over *Flying Scotsman*. Without their approval to run *Flying Scotsman* abroad, all Pegler's plans would come to naught. Hunslet was well-versed in steam locomotives, though, and the officials had nothing to worry about. They gave *Flying Scotsman* their seal of approval and issued her with the precious North American operating permit she would need.

Pegler knew that his plans would cause uproar amongst rail enthusiasts and many others. They had come within weeks of losing *Flying Scotsman* earlier in the 1960s, and, perhaps with echoes of the *Titanic* in mind, some were worried about the potential mishaps that could befall this iconic locomotive on her way to the New World. Others worried that she might end up stranded in the United States, perhaps as a tourist attraction, and never to return to Britain. Pegler announced the trip while *Flying Scotsman* was still being overhauled in early 1969 and moved immediately to counter the concerns, announcing that, while the tour would run in 1969, *Flying Scotsman* would return to Britain in 1970 and continue to run on BR until the main-line contract expired in 1971. After that, he hinted, other foreign tours might be possible, perhaps to Japan and Australia.

Preparations for shipping *Flying Scotsman* moved ahead, and she was given a final fettling up at Doncaster Works in August. There, she was fitted with the brass bell the Americans deemed necessary on the approach to level crossings, and a large hooter on the side of the smokebox, which was rather louder than the classic Gresley whistle fitted above the firebox. She made a test run from Doncaster to Peterborough via Lincoln, and on 31 August hauled a rail tour from King's Cross to Newcastle for the LNER Society. This final tour had the atmosphere of a wake: concerns about the mishaps that might befall *Flying Scotsman* weighed heavily on some of the passengers, and there were those in the crowds thronging the lineside who had misgivings too. Would they ever, they wondered, see *Flying Scotsman* in full cry again?

Two weeks later, after final preparations, *Flying Scotsman* took its administration coach from Doncaster to Edge Hill depot in Liverpool for the final stage of its journey. The other coaches and exhibition vans had been sent to the United States a few days earlier: all that remained was for *Flying Scotsman* to join them. Harold Wilson, the Prime Minister, perhaps mindful of the time he'd been on the footplate, offered his blessings to the exhibition: 'There are tremendous opportunities for exporters who are prepared to follow up the openings created by this venture,' he said.

On 19 September the floating crane *Mammoth* lifted first *Flying Scotsman*, and then her tenders, on to the Cunard freighter *Saxonia*. The imperturbable Pegler admits he had palpitations at the sight of *Flying Scotsman* being lifted like a toy from the dockside: 'Nothing did break, fortunately, but it was certainly a worry: I've never forgotten the sight of it in the air over the ship!'

Her departure was marked with a blaze of publicity. To help promote the train, the famous Scottish pipe-major Robert Crabbe had been recruited to entertain the crowds, as had a group of glamorous young ladies headed by the twenty-one-year-old beauty queen Kathy Leigh, who also acted as Pegler's personal assistant (and became known, inevitably, as 'Miss *Flying Scotsman*'). She and the other girls would act as front-of-house for the exhibition, and provide a welcome glitz to the tour, courtesy of an organisation called

London Stateside, which was to sell souvenirs alongside the train in a pair of converted London buses. Furthermore, Sir Winston Churchill's great-nephew, John Spencer Churchill, was to travel with the train to give the Churchillian connection some real-life credibility; he proved a popular travelling companion. With a skirl of pipes and the girls waving goodbye in front of *Flying Scotsman*'s smokebox, this fanfare added to the blaze of publicity. She was going to America, and by golly, she was going in the glamour to which she had become so accustomed!

On 28 September *Saxonia* anchored in Boston harbour after a safe crossing of the Atlantic. Two floating cranes belonging to the US Navy were used to lift *Flying Scotsman*, and with Crabbe piping away, *Flying Scotsman*, her tenders and the administration coaches were unloaded without event. After extensive checks following her sea voyage, *Flying Scotsman* was reunited with the exhibition train on 3 October and undertook a test run from Boston to New London, Connecticut, that day. Ever the opportunist, Hinchcliffe couldn't resist the opportunity to fire her. Inspecting the train the following day, though, he noticed that springs on two of the exhibition carriages were down. Gingerly entering them, he found to his amazement that they were stacked from floor to ceiling with promotional literature. In his memoirs, he recalls a conversation a BR official had with the Port of Boston Authority 'who claimed that the two cars, which on paper, weighed 30 tonnes each, in fact, according to the crane driver, weighed in at 60 tonnes! The mystery was solved, but I kept quiet,' he said. That day, she backed into Boston South Station to go on parade.

The train was meant to be entirely for business, but the American public had other ideas. Thousands flocked to see her, attracted by the novelty and spectacle of such an unusual sight in their country. Although Britain had just completed the elimination of steam, most of the private railways of the United States had done so long before: 1960 is usually reckoned to be the last significant year of steam operation in the USA, though a number of smaller lines continued beyond then. Furthermore, the rise of the automobile meant that many towns and cities which had once had a rail service were now bereft, their lines, if they hadn't been closed, used exclusively for the gigantic freight trains operated in America. *Flying Scotsman*, then, was a rare sight in every sense.

Hinchcliffe organised it so that the train was free for trade visitors in the mornings and evenings, with the public allowed in during the afternoons. It was a pattern which would work well throughout the tour. But it was another aspect of the tour which worried him: London Stateside seemed hopelessly optimistic. Hinchcliffe did some back-of-an-envelope calculations and realised that this venture, which employed ten girls, would have to take a vast amount to cover its costs.

As the start date of the tour approached, nerves grew: would the reception afforded to her initially be granted everywhere she went, or had America – which that year had landed a man on the moon – advanced too far beyond the steam age to care? There was only one way to find out.

At 7 a.m. on 12 October *Flying Scotsman* stood at Boston South station, her safety valves simmering with pent-up pressure, and a palpable air of anticipation threaded through the train and amongst the onlookers. American observers, astounded by *Flying Scotsman*'s comparatively tiny size, thought she might have problems mounting the grades on her way from Boston to Hartford – and there were worse to come further on in the tour. These concerns weren't helped by a light drizzle that morning, which stood to make the rails as slippery as ice.

Of course, for a locomotive which had hauled far heavier trains during the war, and at speeds far higher than the 50mph maximum imposed throughout the tour, hauling a nine-coach train should be no problem. So it proved. She purred out of the station and on her way south. She surprised the Americans by storming any gradient that could be thrown at her, speed barely slackening in a seemingly effortless demonstration of her power and efficiency. With her burnished apple-green paintwork and glistening chocolate-and-cream coaches trailing behind, she looked magnificent threading her way through the New England countryside, and perfectly happy in her new environment. She arrived in Hartford later that day and, after overnight servicing, continued to New York. *Flying Scotsman* was going on show in the Big Apple.

And she would go on show in some style. She was to be displayed at the all-electric Penn Station, now underneath Madison Square Gardens (Grand Central would surely have been a more spectacular venue, but this proved impossible to arrange). She was hauled into the station by an electric locomotive to prevent undue pollution, both to comply with local laws and also because the station platforms were underground. She was there for four days, and again, thousands flocked to see her. The tour had got off to a promising start.

Rich Taylor saw her in Penn Station and on her journey from New York:

> My impression at the time was that *Flying Scotsman* was a prim lady compared with American locomotives.
>
> Even after I went along the four-track main line to see the train pass, there was little locomotive sound due to the level track and 40mph speed restriction: it wasn't until my first UK trip that I realised British locomotives will match, if not surpass the sound of many of the locomotives here. To this day I find it difficult to believe the train was figuratively speaking in my back yard almost thirty-eight years ago!

Within days of the tour, though, rumours were circulating that London Stateside wasn't able to pay hotel bills for the girls. Hinchcliffe investigated further: 'It didn't take me long to realise it was impossible to get sufficient numbers of people through the buses to take much more than $100 or so per hour,' he wrote. Hinchcliffe reckoned that getting people in England to part with more than £1 for a souvenir was tricky, but nothing on the buses was under $5, and according to Hinchcliffe, most items were over $10.

The train left New York for Washington DC by way of

Philadelphia and Baltimore, where a regulator gland failed, as did the brick arch in the firebox, a casualty of the fiercely burning American coal. Worse still, by this point, as Hinchcliffe had feared, London Stateside went bust. It looked as if the girls – a great promotional tool for the train – would be sent home. Hinchcliffe was told that Pegler had taken over the souvenir side, and that the girls would instead work for *Flying Scotsman* Enterprises (which would operate the locomotive on Pegler's behalf). It was extra work for Hinchcliffe, and he asked if his wife, Frances, could come over to help. Pegler, who recognised the importance of Hinchcliffe to the venture, agreed readily.

The mishaps were recoverable, however, and the train arrived in the capital on 25 October. Here, the Americans surpassed themselves. So popular was *Flying Scotsman* that crowds queued for more than three hours to inspect the train and see just how differently the British had evolved their steam locomotives.

From Washington DC, which she left on 28 October, *Flying Scotsman* continued her journey to her hosts, the Southern Railway. Claytor, now president of the railway, was a lifelong steam enthusiast who had kept in working order the mixed-traffic locomotive No. 4501. He'd been planning a special welcome for *Flying Scotsman* in the Deep South: it would be perhaps the most memorable part of the tour.

On November 2, she steamed towards the medium-sized Alabama city of Anniston. At the same time, Claytor's Pacific, No. 4501, hauled a special train from Birmingham,

Alabama, and finally the Atlanta Chapter of the National Railway Historical Society sent its preserved freight loco- motive, No. 750, to join the other two. It would be a spectacular meeting. The three locomotives and their trains met appropriately at high noon, and after a series of photographic run-pasts, were positioned in a freight yard for display. The difference between British and American practice could not have been starker. Though quite a giant by British standards, *Flying Scotsman* was simply dwarfed by her American counterparts, even though they were only what the Americans would deem medium-sized engines. *Flying Scotsman*'s pipework was elegantly hidden, and many American enthusiasts used the term 'toy-like' – not in any pejorative sense, but, as Brian Haresnape wrote, 'in amaze- ment that something so fine and delicate of line, so perfect in finish and polish, so model-like in appearance, could actually exist in real life.' The Americans were stunned, and between 3,000 and 5,000 people flocked to see *Flying Scotsman* that day. Claytor addressed the crowd, whom he told tongue-in- cheek that the Southern would indeed continue to run steam locomotives, but that there was no truth in the scurrilous rumour that it was going to replace its modern diesels with their older counterparts! Pegler loved the occasion, dressed in his overalls and sunglasses, and he thanked the Southern Railway for hosting *Flying Scotsman* and for finally allowing an LNER locomotive to visit America.

The ceremony over, *Flying Scotsman* continued her journey to Birmingham, and among those treated to a cab ride was the editor of the US enthusiast magazine *Trains*,

David P Morgan. He gushed with enthusiasm: 'One glance at 4472 told one that she was a lady, an accredited member of mechanical high society . . . every visible inch of her metal bespoke a craftsmanship of construction seldom known in our rough and ready railroading.' It was high praise indeed from a man respected across the USA as an expert.

Reaction across America was almost universally positive – in the town of Cuba, a school class was dismissed early and taken to the tracks to wave at this glamorous foreign train. Elsewhere, enthusiasts travelled thousands of miles to get a glimpse – and, of course, there were many unsuspecting people taken completely by surprise at the sight and sound of a foreign steam locomotive hauling a passenger train through their towns.

For the staff, it must have been an amazing experience. Pegler was feted by the American media, who took immediately to his polished accent and slightly raffish demeanour. They also took to the girls, who found themselves a star attraction wherever they went – almost as much as the locomotive! The parties in the observation car of an evening must have been fantastic, with the ever-charismatic Pegler holding forth in the observation saloon, and a ready and seemingly inexhaustible supply of refreshments. It was a once-in-a-lifetime opportunity for everyone, and they made the most of it.

Flying Scotsman and her entourage reached Dallas on 4 November, and then her last tour destination, Houston, on 10 November. The owner, drivers and firemen, as well as the support staff including the ten models, were treated to a civic reception to mark the end of the thirty-nine-day tour. Pegler's last brilliant stunt was to get the astronaut Al Worden to light the fire of *Flying Scotsman* shortly before he flew to the moon on the *Apollo 15* mission. Worden also lit another fire, becoming smitten with Miss *Flying Scotsman* herself, Kathy Leigh. Who says the romance of rail travel is dead?

From Houston, the tour over, *Flying Scotsman* worked the 400 miles to Slaton, Texas, where she and her coaches were stored undercover in a roundhouse for the winter. It was time to take stock: *Flying Scotsman* had been visited, it is reckoned, by 60,000 people, each paying one dollar each. Many exhibitors had taken substantial orders, and a huge amount of goodwill had been generated, both for *Flying Scotsman* and for Britain. However, it was also an expensive tour to operate, with legal fees and running fees for operating on all but the Santa Fe railroad, and the costs of salaries and staff accommodation – for they all had to be put up in pre-booked motels. Financially, it had only just broken even, but, as Pegler flew home for Christmas, he could justifiably feel pleased with a job well done: so much so that he planned to continue the tour in 1970.

Pegler went to see the Board of Trade, expecting, if not a red carpet, then at least a hearty welcome. He was to be disappointed. 'Their reaction wasn't "Well done old chap; jolly good show for flying the flag," but an extremely lukewarm one, which indicated there would be no further support.' Just as Beeching felt that steam would damage the image of British Railways, so the Board of Trade now felt that *Flying Scotsman* would make foreigners think that Britain was an old-fashioned nation which still ran steam locomotives. Even though the Board of Trade was getting requests from companies to be involved, it seemed it was doing its utmost to dissuade them. It looked like the tour would have to be cancelled, and that *Flying Scotsman* would have to return home.

What really persuaded Pegler to try and find a way of making it happen was a major change of heart by the American operating authorities. Though he'd had a few unofficial turns at driving *Flying Scotsman* in America, it was only when he was discussing arrangements for the second tour that a senior official turned to face him and said: 'You own the engine; you'd better drive the goddamn thing!'

Pegler was dumbfounded: 'I couldn't believe my ears,' he admitted: 'After all the red tape on Britain's railways, here was I, a member of the public, being invited to drive a Gresley Pacific at speed for thousands of miles through some of the most majestic scenery in the world!'

For a man like Pegler, there was only one possible thing to do: 'It was my every wish come true, and, although I knew the money was in danger of running out, I said to myself "My God, I'm never going to have this opportunity again, so I'm going to make the most of it for as long as I can and face the music later. If I go broke, I'll just have to work for a living!"'

New displays were organised for the carriages, including, bizarrely, a set of Gilbert and Sullivan models, a collection of original costumes from the British film *Anne of the Thousand*

Days, a model railway layout, British textiles, and an exhibit by the Midwest Railways Society of Chicago that was virtually a mobile museum in itself. It was far removed from the big business of the previous year's train.

The plan for the second tour was to run from Slaton, Texas, via Dallas, Fort Worth, Kansas City, St Louis and Chicago, finally arriving in Green Bay for the National Railway Museum on 19 July. One of the Pullman coaches was dropped off there, and *Flying Scotsman* spent a month on display in company with a close cousin – the streamlined A4 Pacific *Dwight D Eisenhower*, which had been presented by the British government to the museum at the end of steam – moved on into Canada, where she visited a number of cities. She was stored in the huge roundhouse at Spadina, Toronto for the bitter winter.

The tour hadn't passed without mishap. The bearings on one of the Pullman cars, *Isle of Thanet*, ran hot, so it was with some sense of relief that it was dropped off at Green Bay. More seriously, though, the trailing wheels of the locomotive were damaged as it traversed a crossover on its way north. The bearing was damaged severely, and there was no option other than to remove the wheels and machine it. Throughout the blazing-hot afternoon and into the night, the cab-end of *Flying Scotsman* was lifted, and the wheelset sent to Santa Fe's workshops in Cleburne some 220 miles away at 2 a.m. the next morning. In a remarkable feat, the repaired wheelset was completed and installed by the end of the following day.

Throughout the second tour, the financial situation

became increasingly precarious. Though Hinchcliffe, by now a full-time paid member of the team, tried all his wiles to raise funds, when it came to getting what he called 'dollars that one can actually see and feel', support drained away. Despite this, Pegler revelled in driving his locomotive for mile after mile. It was a childhood dream come true, and he wanted to eke it out as long as he could.

By the time the train reached Ottawa, however, the venture was in trouble. Half the staff were sent home to try and save costs, and worse still, while *Flying Scotsman* was kept securely under cover, the carriages were left outside to weather the harsh Canadian winter. Back in England, the Board of Trade had become the Department of Trade & Industry, and it was adamant that it wasn't going to support what was looking increasingly like a reckless adventure. 'I hope they were satisfied,' said a bitter Pegler: 'because I ended up £132,000 in debt.'

There were real worries now about the future of *Flying Scotsman*, and with good reason. Pegler knew that he would almost certainly become bankrupt, but there was, he felt, the tiniest glimmer of hope. The city of San Francisco was to hold a British Week in 1971, and if, somehow, *Flying Scotsman* could get there, it was just possible that the commercial situation might be turned around. It was worth a go. Canadian National, which had stored the locomotive over winter, agreed to release *Flying Scotsman* in return for a percentage of the takings from the journey across America.

Crewing problems reared their ugly head as Pegler tried

to keep costs down. He could drive, but for the most part, there just three others for the onerous and demanding footplate tasks. One thing they were never without, though was goodwill, and volunteers galore turned up to help: even doing mundane tasks like cleaning, cooking and taking tickets would lighten the load on the full-time staff. But expertise in operating steam railways was rare in North America, so inevitably much of the burden fell on the British contingent.

From Joliet, on the outskirts of Chicago, to San Francisco, the train's progress became something more like an epic expedition. Photographers, students, industrialists, girls on their way home to California, all became part of the train crew, and all were given regular tasks. Only on the footplate did the professionals (and, of course, Pegler and Hinchcliffe) really hold sway. Getting coal proved another problem. Though the railways on whose tracks *Flying Scotsman* ran did their best to help, all too often they hedged their bets on the financial situation and demanded that the coal was paid for as it was obtained. And the quality got steadily worse as *Flying Scotsman* went further west, with stops to raise steam becoming an irritatingly frequent occurrence. Lack of maintenance facilities also proved a challenge, with much improvisation needed to keep her running: with no ready supply of spares, and using completely different components to American locomotives, *Flying Scotsman*'s survival depended on her reliability.

Kevin Bunker was just one of many US rail enthusiasts compelled to go trackside to welcome 4472 to Northern

California and the Bay Area. He was about sixteen at the time, but more than thirty-five years on, it left a vivid impression with him:

I had not, until that moment, seen live mainline steam of any kind, having been born just before Southern Pacific Company dropped the fires in the last of its steam power in the later 1950s. It seemed a bit odd, to be sure, that a three-cylinder Gresley compound from the UK on the Western Pacific Railroad (of all roads) would be my first experience, but there you are.

Joining several friends from the Bay Area, we chased south from Sacramento (my hometown) to see 4472 leave the South Sacramento yards, which was rather underwhelming. Figuring we could not catch it anywhere on the way to Stockton, we simply dashed all the way to the latter city and waited trackside for the special train to approach the Santa Fe Railway-Western Pacific diamond crossing. In due course, 4472 and train made its way into Stockton, its borrowed Southern Railway brass chime whistle announcing its passage across the numerous level crossings along the way.

She was moving so slowly due to the crowds around the passenger depot that we continued to be surprised that the locomotive seemed to lack 'presence' – a throaty voice at the chimney, if you will. Of course, we still had not yet seen the engine really work, let alone sprint at track speed. Suddenly, 4472 was given clearance to cross another line and she burst forward with the distinctive Gresley loping exhaust. Those far older than me who recalled Southern

Pacific's Gresley-design Alco 4-10-2s would have remembered that off-centre exhaust beat, but it certainly surprised my ears!

We dashed to our car as the locomotive passed to try and make our way further west to some point where we could see the old girl really fly, but could not catch the train at French Camp below Stockton, such were the crowds and traffic on adjacent highways. We jumped onto the westbound interstate highway leading toward Altamont Pass and decided our best bet was to make it to the pass ahead of the train. Little did we know that 4472 was running short of coal and that the heavy Altamont grade would tax her fireman. It was (and still is) my understanding that working hard up Altamont, she ran starved for steam and quite simply ran very nearly out of coal. We could hear, in the far distance, the locomotive hammering its way slowly up the mountain until its sound dissipated. Eventually she came almost painfully slowly round the bend past the summit and ground to a halt. And there she was forced to wait for the arrival of a diesel to assist her and the train the rest of the way into Oakland. We rejoined the hobbled 4472 at West Oakland, and it was there that my then new friend, railroad photographer Ted Benson, snapped a very artful backlit photograph of me and 4472 in the late afternoon sun.

I hoped to see 4472 operating in San Francisco on the port railroad, but on the one day I did visit, she was on static display. On that occasion, though, I managed to get a few minutes with Alan Pegler in the former 'Devon Belle' observation car, after which, he conducted me through the train and the corridor tenders up into 4472's footplate and cab. I was a budding railway artist in those years, and brought as a gift a recent sketch I'd made of a West Side Lumber Company Shay locomotive – a curious choice on my part, but which utterly charmed Alan, who from that moment became a friend. We corresponded off and on for some years until he retired to Wales, after which we lost touch.

She and the A3 locomotives were clearly a breed apart and a most remarkable series of able locomotives, and I was pleased to have her be the representative that led me to learn more about Gresley and the London & North Eastern Railway.

Bunker's enthusiasm is a typical illustration of the lengths rail enthusiasts will go to pursue their passion, and he wasn't alone. James L Powell was one of the visitors the year before at Dallas:

At that time a live steam locomotive was a most unusual sight. The last steam locomotive I saw in operation was at the Reader Railroad in Arkansas in 1965, and I certainly wanted to view *Flying Scotsman* first-hand and make a movie of it. I remember making comparisons between it and the static American steam locomotives that I was familiar with at the Texas State Fair Park exhibit. I remember how the styling differed from the US locomotives. The next day I filmed her, and *Flying Scotsman* put on a good show for me and the others stationed to watch her go by. All too soon, it was gone!

As the end of September 1971 approached, *Flying Scotsman* and her train were given a refresh to prepare them for British Week, and on 27 September she finally arrived at Fisherman's Wharf in San Francisco. At this point, control was handed over to *Flying Scotsman* Enterprises to try and make enough money to repatriate this iconic locomotive. Fisherman's Wharf was just long enough for a seven-coach train, so one of the windowless exhibition cars had been left behind en route. Things were now getting really desperate financially, with the staff sleeping aboard the train and, every three or four nights, a motel room being hired. The crew took it in turns to use the shower and wash their socks and pants. A different person would sleep in the room each night, chosen by a rota.

Pegler was being chased by creditors, and at one point, a writ was even slapped on *Flying Scotsman*'s buffer beam. Pegler ripped it off, but it was a near thing. Promised sponsorship had failed to materialise, and as a final punch in the face, although the authorities were prepared to let *Flying Scotsman* stay on Fisherman's Wharf for six months, they would only do so if they were compensated for the loss of revenue from the ninety-three parking meters it occupied. It cost Pegler £1,000 per week, but amazingly, she made a profit, so great were the crowds wanting to walk though the train and corridor tender. One unusual visitor was the singer Tom Jones, then at the height of his fame, and for six months from September 1971, *Flying Scotsman* was one of the most popular tourist attractions, if not the most popular, in a city not short of them.

The train became a popular venue for business meetings, corporate entertaining and social functions, and if she had been allowed to remain there, it seems likely that enough money would have been made to pay off Pegler's debts and repatriate the locomotive. However, the local businesses on Fisherman's Wharf felt they were losing business because there was nowhere for potential customers to park, and *Flying Scotsman* was ordered to move to the other end of the quay.

This initially seemed like a good move, because after much negotiation with safety authorities, Hinchcliffe and Pegler won permission to operate two-mile shuttle trips on the San Francisco Belt Railroad, making *Flying Scotsman* the first and only British train to carry fare-paying passengers on a US railway. This started off well and, with fares priced at $3 return, seemed to make money, but it soon proved a false dawn. Speed was limited to just 10mph, thanks to all the level crossings and the constant bell-ringing the locomotive had to do, and the smoke and noise soon caused complaints from locals. But the final nail in the coffin was that *Flying Scotsman* was out of the public eye. The spontaneous tourist trade evaporated, and within just a few weeks of the first run on 14 March, Pegler was staring bankruptcy straight in the face.

Although he could have stayed in the US and avoided it, because his son Tim was a permanent resident of the US, he opted to return to Britain to sort out his, and the locomotive's future. He was bought a return ticket by one of *Flying Scotsman*'s American supporters and, after filing for bankruptcy in July 1972, he returned to see what could be done to save his beloved engine. For *Flying Scotsman*, it was as dark an hour as in January 1963, when she had been due to be withdrawn by British Railways. This time, though, there was no knight in shining armour waiting in the wings.

Hinchcliffe came to the fore and arranged for *Flying Scotsman* and her train to be stored at the Sharpe Army base: a place creditors would find hard to enter, and one which offered secure storage. In light steam, and hauled by a diesel, she left San Francisco on 13 August 1972. As the crew put *Flying Scotsman* to bed and disbanded, it looked as if the fires had gone out forever. Hinchcliffe resumed his career in teaching, and Pegler, financially ruined by the engine he had done so much to save and keep running, sat down on Fisherman's Wharf, scratched his head, and said: 'What on earth do I do now?'

Chapter Twelve
Rescue!

While Alan Pegler sat on Fisherman's Wharf in San Francisco pondering his next move, concern was growing in Britain about the fate of *Flying Scotsman*. By a cruel irony, three of *Flying Scotsman* Enterprises' principal creditors were railway companies. There was to be no solidarity with their British debtor. *Flying Scotsman* was the principal asset, and they, and the other creditors, wanted to recover as much of their costs as possible.

It didn't take long for momentum to build up in Britain to save it, led by Alan Bloom, one of the pioneering railway preservationists. Bloom, a horticulturalist, ran Bressingham Gardens in Norfolk, and was busy establishing a railway centre as an added attraction. He had bought some small tank engines, but he also had custodianship of British Railways' last steam locomotive to haul a passenger train, the Britannia-class Pacific *Oliver Cromwell*. He formed a committee to try and repatriate *Flying Scotsman*, and one of his first acts was to call his friend, and fellow locomotive-owner, William McAlpine, of the construction company.

McAlpine, then in his thirties, had long been a steam enthusiast and, after a spell of national service in the 1950s, had continued to work his way through the ranks of the

McAlpine company. He had bought *Flying Scotsman*'s great rival, *Pendennis Castle*, with Lord Gretton and was also starting to build up a collection of steam traction engines and locomotives at his home in Buckinghamshire. He was well-off, and might be in a position to help the public appeal to save *Flying Scotsman* that was envisaged.

McAlpine is a rather modest man not given to boasting, but his enthusiasm for railways is beyond doubt. (Mike Wild – one of my biggest helpers in writing this book – and I went to visit Sir William at his home in Buckinghamshire, and interviewed him in his library.) He was born on 12 January 1936 at London's Dorchester Hotel, but he wasn't excused working for the family company, starting as an apprentice at the age of sixteen. On his first day he was given some tools and an engine and told to dismantle it – and then to reassemble it, so he would know how it worked. His eventual high position was won on merit, not birthright. National service saw him join the army, but his upbringing hadn't prepared him for fatigue duty. Confronted with a sack of potatoes and a peeler, a Liverpool soldier watched him with growing curiosity before saying: 'Ain't you ever peeled a spud before, sir?'

'Well, no, actually,' responded McAlpine. Shortly after, a coin changed hands, and, as Sir William recalls, he never did peel a potato in the army!

Though for a man of his wealth Sir William doesn't have the gigantic mansion some might imagine, the library is magnificent. The shelves are stacked with books, and the wall space between is covered in railway paintings and drawings. And then there's his collection of railway arte-facts. He is widely reckoned to have the biggest collection outside the National Railway Museum, and it encompasses a number of sheds full to the rafters of everything from furniture to signs, to models and nameplates. Best of all, though, is the railway in the grounds of his house. Sir William has built from new a running line of around a mile in length complete with stations, signal box and level crossing. The locomotive, a small saddle tank, was the last steam locomotive used by the family firm, Sir Robert McAlpine.

Before the committee could do much, however, shocking news came from the United States: three railway companies which were creditors were working together to try and seize *Flying Scotsman* and her coaches to sell for as much money as possible. Action was needed urgently, and as soon as he found out, Bloom called McAlpine: 'Alan Bloom gave me a ring to say, "We are here, and *Flying Scotsman*'s in trouble. We think we ought to get together and do something." And I said, "Well the only thing to do is get hold of George Hinchcliffe," ' recalls McAlpine.

Although Hinchcliffe was now back teaching, McAlpine, who had seen *Flying Scotsman* in San Francisco, knew well that he was the best person to sort things out. McAlpine agreed to pay Hinchcliffe's fare to Washington DC to meet the lawyers and waited patiently for him to get back in touch. Hinchcliffe arrived on 30 December 1972 and called the lawyer Bill Mann. Mann gave him the bad news that the creditors were now actively seeking the court order that would give them custody of *Flying Scotsman*. He was sceptical of McAlpine (though when he learned that McAlpine was born in London's Dorchester Hotel, he became more reasonable). The railway creditors were unwilling to allow more time for a deal to be sorted, so McAlpine and Hinchcliffe would have to work quickly.

McAlpine asked Hinchcliffe if he could arrange the move back to Britain, and Hinchcliffe said yes. By an incredible coincidence, Hinchcliffe had sat next to a man who worked for a shipping line in San Francisco called Johnson Scanstar. Hinchcliffe explained his problems, told him where he could be located in San Francisco (where he had flown to see friends) and never really expected to hear from him again. To his surprise, there was a message awaiting him after a meeting: 'I have a ship sailing in 14 days – please phone.' Hinchcliffe did, and he agreed a price before calling McAlpine to confirm that he could arrange *Flying Scotsman*'s shipment home.

McAlpine hesitated before asking his second question: 'If you get it back, will you run it for me and manage it?' Hinchcliffe replied that he would have to ask his wife Frances, but she readily agreed. 'With that, all I could say was "yes",' thought McAlpine. The funds were transferred in the nick of time for just half the amount the railroads wanted: finally, it looked as if *Flying Scotsman*'s future was secure – although Hinchcliffe remained twitchy about some hitherto unknown creditor suddenly appearing.

Western Pacific Railroad was understandably reluctant to get involved with *Flying Scotsman* once more, but, after the promise of payment in advance, agreed to move her from Sharpe Army base to San Francisco Docks, where she would be lifted on to barges, and then on to the ship that was to take her home, the *California Star*. To Hinchcliffe's horror, it now appeared that the San Francisco Port Authority was one of the creditors: was everything to fall apart at the last minute? 'Here we were right in the lion's den, and, to make things worse, we had a reporter anxious to catch the evening's edition!' he remembers.

There was only one thing to do with a nosy reporter: ply him with scotch. Hinchcliffe made sure the reporter was so drunk there was no way he could file copy, and, once *Flying Scotsman* was safely, securely and irrecoverably loaded, he went to meet Pegler (who was still in San Francisco) and give him the good news: *Flying Scotsman* was coming home, with her second tender – but the coaches and exhibition vans would be left behind.

Reflecting on it later, McAlpine said: 'I think it was almost my patriotic duty. I did feel that it needed to be saved, and it should be brought home. Somebody ought to do it, and that stage I didn't really know how it would be done, whether other people would want to join in, or what. But then the die was cast. George got it home.'

McAlpine was the one person in Britain in a position to save *Flying Scotsman*, given the time constraints imposed by the American creditors. His generosity – and, crucially, his decisiveness – ensured that, rather than ending up stuffed and mounted at somewhere like Long Beach, home of such retired transport icons as the liner *Queen Mary* and the

'Spruce Goose' flying boat (this was a real possibility at the time), the locomotive would have a future in Britain. He soon bought it from Pegler for what Pegler calls 'a song', and then *Flying Scotsman* was his to do whatever he wanted with. Intriguingly, a very short article was published in *The Railway Magazine* after the deal had been sealed, saying that the locomotive was to be donated to the National Collection. Given McAlpine's desire to see *Flying Scotsman* running, and for George Hinchcliffe to manage it, one wonders whether this was mere journalistic wishful thinking. Certainly, nothing more was heard of this plan. It didn't matter: McAlpine's sound business sense meant that there was to be no repeat of the American adventure.

The journey from San Francisco to Liverpool via the Panama Canal was a rough one. The *California Star* was hit by the terrifying force of an Atlantic gale, but thankfully, *Flying Scotsman* had been extremely securely fastened to the deck, and survived without damage. She arrived back at Liverpool on 13 February 1973 to a rapturous reception. The floating crane unloaded her, and McAlpine sat on the fireman's seat: 'This engine is mine – I don't believe it! I never really felt like I owned her,' he confided.

Now that she had landed in Britain, McAlpine intended to send *Flying Scotsman* to BR's Derby Works for a much-needed overhaul. It was hoped that she could make the journey under her own steam, but in order for that to happen, British Rail needed to be sure that storage in America and the sea voyage hadn't left her unfit for service. She certainly looked work-stained, but that would mean little to British Rail's diligent inspectors, all of whom remembered steam well. They were satisfied she would be fine to continue – and in fact, she still had some really high-quality coal from Utah in her tender – but the final decision was up to the regional manager, Dick Hardy. Hardy was one of the greatest operating men ever to work on the railways, and he was also an out-and-out steam man. There was no way he would refuse permission for *Flying Scotsman* to run to Derby under her own steam if his inspectors agreed that she was in good enough condition to make it: it was a momentous decision.

Once again *Flying Scotsman* was headline news, as amidst euphoria she steamed proudly to Derby. It was like a royal visit, with the lineside all the way thronged with well-wishers overjoyed to see her back. A flight of Royal Air Force Phantom fighter-bombers even saluted her as she steamed eastwards. The only thing missing was the sound of church bells ringing to mark the homecoming.

At Derby, *Flying Scotsman* had her American accoutrements taken off. The unsightly hooter and headlamp bracket were removed, as was the bell. She was stripped down and emerged repainted in the apple green that suited her so well. She was launched – and what a change of heart this demonstrated – by British Rail's Chairman, Richard Marsh, before heading to her new home in Devon.

British Rail's steam ban, which meant that, other than *Flying Scotsman*, no other steam locomotives were able to operate on the national network, had proved short-lived. One of the National Collection's most popular steam locomotives, the Great Western's gigantic 4-6-0 *King George V*, had been kept in steam by the cider makers Bulmers in Hereford, where she hauled short demonstration trains on the company's sidings. Peter Prior of Bulmers wanted to use the locomotive on a promotional train, and after lengthy negotiations, in October 1971 – the year Pegler's agreement with BR expired – *King George V* was on a special train which included a couple of carriages for fare-paying passengers. The run was a massive success, and, having seen the goodwill it generated, BR relented. The steam ban was over, just three years after the end of main-line steam operation. There were caveats – steam operation was banned in the summer because of the fire risk, and just six short routes were cleared – but it was a start, and it meant that the giants of steam would be able to stretch their legs properly.

By the time *Flying Scotsman* emerged from Derby it was July 1973, which meant that she wouldn't be able to earn her crust on the main line. However, while she had been in America, something truly remarkable had happened that meant that whatever the policy regarding main-line steam, there would always be a railway for *Flying Scotsman* to run on: the railway preservation movement was building up a head of steam that continues to this day.

The Beeching cuts of the 1960s were so extensive that in many cases, lines were closed and simply allowed to rot rather than being demolished, and that gave a brief window of opportunity to resurrect old lines. In the 1950s the Ealing comedy *The Titfield Thunderbolt* had made fun of the idea of a bunch of eccentrics trying to keep their line open, but by the late 1960s and early 1970s the notion was widespread enough for ridicule to evaporate. An idea hitherto restricted by sheer practicality to the narrow-gauge railways of Wales suddenly exploded into reality on the standard-gauge lines of England, Wales and Scotland. The first was the Middleton Railway in Leeds at the end of the 1950s, closely followed by the Bluebell Railway in Sussex, but it was really from the mid-1960s that some of the most famous names in railway preservation got going. The North Yorkshire Moors Railway from Grosmont to Pickering; the Keighley & Worth Valley Railway; the Severn Valley Railway; what is now called the Paignton & Dartmouth Steam Railway – all had their genesis in the 1960s, and by 1973 all were carrying passengers. There were others too, in varying states of completion.

A number of wealthy individuals and groups had bought engines directly from British Rail: mostly big express types, but also mixed-traffic types including a former LNER B1, and a number of the steadfast 'Black Fives' introduced by the LMS in the 1930s. These provided some of the motive power for the embryonic heritage railways, as did industrial locomotives bought from companies upgrading to diesel traction. The biggest spur of all, though, came from a forgotten scrapyard in Wales.

In the 1960s the scrap merchant Dai Woodham bought hundreds of steam locomotives, carriages and wagons from British Railways. He concentrated on the carriages and wagons first, as they were easier to break up, and, as business was good, he was content to leave the steam locomotives to gently rust away until a quieter time. It didn't take long for word to get out amongst enthusiasts that there were something like 200 steam locomotives in a scrapyard in Barry, and it didn't take long either for groups to start buying them from Woodham and begin the lengthy process of restoration. It was Dai Woodham whom we have to thank for the survival of a number of unique types, including the last passenger locomotive built by British Railways, No. 71000 *Duke of Gloucester*. This combination of closed lines and a ready (at a price) source of motive power really secured the future of railway preservation at a time when some wondered about its appeal.

McAlpine decided to send *Flying Scotsman* to run on the Torbay Steam Railway for the summer season of 1973 after her overhaul at Derby. The line runs from Paignton to Kingswear in glorious Devon. She hauled McAlpine's immaculate pair of inspection saloons from Derby without difficulty, and settled in to a ten-week season hauling tourist trains on this picturesque little line, doing five return trips daily for four days a week. She proved a huge attraction, both with passengers and staff. There was, almost inevitably, some friendly regional rivalry between the Great Western loyalists of the Torbay Steam Railway and *Flying Scotsman*'s own crew. One day she was rostered to haul a thirteen-coach train from Paignton, assisted by the GWR Manor-class *Lydham Manor*. *Flying Scotsman*'s supporters claimed the locomotive would take the coaches and *Lydham Manor* single-handed. The Manor's crew said their engine could do the same in the opposite direction. The gauntlet was laid down, and without further ado, *Flying Scotsman* strolled away with her train, probably equivalent to something like fifteen coaches with the added dead weight of *Lydham Manor*. At the steepest point on the line, the safety valves started to lift, sure proof that *Flying Scotsman* had plenty in hand.

On the return journey, *Lydham Manor* gamely struggled with her heavy load, but as the speed came down to just 10mph, her crew had to finally acknowledge that they needed help from the bigger engine if they were to keep time. Game, set and match to *Flying Scotsman*, albeit against a much smaller and less powerful engine.

As summer turned to autumn, main-line steam again became practical, and on 22 September *Flying Scotsman* teamed up with *King George V* to haul a train from Newport to Shrewsbury. The train was appropriately named 'The Atlantic Venturers Express', and it was the first time that two British locomotives that had visited America hauled the same train. The reception involved the usual crowds: anyone who wondered whether *Flying Scotsman* really was back and on form knew for certain now! The pair savaged the steep gradients on this line, making them appear almost as if they weren't there: these were two locomotives on the very top of their game.

Because *King George V* was too wide and tall for some routes, *Flying Scotsman* was used to haul the Bulmers promotional train in the north of England. Of course, her corridor tender meant that when she was on display, people could enter her cab, and then walk through the corridor tender to the train. She was as popular as ever, but McAlpine and Hinchcliffe knew that the present *ad hoc* arrangements would have to be replaced by something more permanent. *Flying Scotsman* was moved to a shed at Market Overton near Grantham on a branch line serving an iron-ore quarry, where McAlpine's other big engine, *Pendennis Castle*, was maintained. It was appropriate the two locomotives should be stabled together given their shared history. The pair worked a number of rail tours together, and on runs between Newport and Shrewsbury *Flying Scotsman* proved just how much more efficient the higher-pressure boiler and better valves fitted in 1947 were. Even though she had to haul her second tender, her coal consumption was less than *Pendennis Castle*'s: eight per cent less, according to Hinchcliffe.

Difficulties in extracting the iron ore at Market Overton meant that the mine's closure was inevitable, but it was only when British Rail wanted to ease the curve on the main line at High Dyke to allow higher speeds, and demanded £100,000 to reinstate the connection to the Market Overton branch that McAlpine and Hinchcliffe decided they had to move *Flying Scotsman* and *Pendennis Castle*. The location they chose was the old steam shed at Carnforth, Lancashire. Carnforth was, and is, unique: it was operational on the last day of BR steam in 1968, and is probably the last 'modern' steam depot in the country. Its gigantic coaling stage and comprehensive facilities made it an ideal base for the burgeoning main-line steam movement. It was also close to the Cumbrian Coast line and the lines from Leeds to Carnforth and from Guide Bridge to Sheffield – three of the few lines steam was allowed to operate on – and therefore made an ideal base for *Flying Scotsman* and her ilk.

Meanwhile, BR was extending permission to operate steam locomotives on the national network only on a yearly basis, something that McAlpine was increasingly concerned about, given the high cost of overhauls and maintenance. So he took British Rail's Bob Reid for lunch and in his usual diplomatic way, made the case for a longer period of steam operation than a year:

> I said to him, 'Look, it's all very well – thank you very much for one year, but if you are going to spend £100,000 overhauling a locomotive [which is the sort of money it was then], you can't write it off in a year.'
>
> 'We do realise your difficulty. We'd like to run it more, but the problem *you've* got is that every nutter in the world wants to run their engine on the main line, to the detriment of everything else. So we will form an association and do a deal with you that all requests come through that association. In return we can run on limited routes by agreement.'

McAlpine floated an idea which seems to have come from the ever-inventive mind of Hinchcliffe: a kind of co-operative among steam locomotive owners to divide the main-line work there was, and to form a single point of contact between the owners and BR. It became known as the Steam Locomotive Owners' Association (SLOA), and it was to prove highly successful.

With main-line steam now virtually guaranteed a secure future on British Rail, main-line work continued for *Flying Scotsman*, and she was an ever-popular draw. In 1976 she was led by the venerable London & North Western Railway 2-4-0 express passenger engine *Hardwicke* – some fifty years older than *Flying Scotsman* – over the picturesque Settle to Carlisle line to mark the route's centenary. Filming appearances in disguise ensured 1977 was interesting to her supporters, and after an overhaul by Vickers at Barrow-in-Furness, where she was fitted with her spare boiler, she hauled two special trains in memory of the great railway photographer, the Rt Revd Eric Treacy, the Bishop of Wakefield, who died on Appleby station while watching his beloved steam locomotives. *Flying Scotsman* was an appropriate locomotive, and the commemorations were well-received, both by BR and the public.

Amazingly, that year, British Rail decided to resume operation of steam *itself*. It hired *Flying Scotsman* to work the Cumbrian Coast Express, a special train aimed at holiday-makers in the area, from Carnforth to Sellafield and back. Sellafield might not have been the most obvious destination, but the scenery is beautiful, and there was a miniature railway, the Ravenglass & Eskdale, too. The trains proved highly popular, but only ran for two years.

Flying Scotsman had a steady workflow and a wealthy backer determined to run her as a business rather than an indulgence, as reflected by the fact that – unlike Pegler, who took every opportunity to travel behind her – McAlpine remained dedicated to his family business. That didn't stop the Inland Revenue chasing McAlpine to try and extract more money from him, however: 'The tax people tried to prove that it was a hobby, so that any losses *Flying Scotsman* incurred wouldn't be set against income tax.' It was a reasonable enough concern, but they made too many unwarranted assumptions: surely the owner of *Flying Scotsman* would be on it all the time – wouldn't he? McAlpine proved that, in that particular year, he had travelled behind *Flying Scotsman* just three times. After all, as he points out: 'I was working and the job came first, and my family came first as well.' And *Flying Scotsman* was doing extremely well with Hinchcliffe and the dedicated support crew behind it. 'I've never been particularly excited by driving it,' says McAlpine. 'I would much rather sit in the saloon at the back and hear the sounds and take in the smell. Actually I want to see the thing properly.'

As the 1970s turned into the 1980s, *Flying Scotsman* continued her main-line and occasional promotional work, and, as it saw the benefits of main-line steam, British Rail gradually widened the number of routes steam locomotives were allowed to operate on. In 1983, to mark *Flying Scotsman*'s sixtieth anniversary, she was exhibited at the National Railway Museum in York, and the following day travelled solo to Doncaster and then to Peterborough to haul a special train back to York. It was a time of celebration, but it almost marked the end for main-line steam. As *Flying Scotsman* approached Stoke Bank, near Grantham, some of the crowd thronging the lineside encroached on to the line to get a better view, or more likely, picture. It was stupid and dangerous. And things were to get worse further north. Having negotiated Grantham without incident, *Flying Scotsman* approached Newark eagerly. Very soon however, the crowds got out of control, thronging on to the East Coast Main Line – a line with a maximum speed in places of 125mph. The police in attendance had little choice: for the trespassers' own safety, they were forced to close the line for fifteen minutes to clear the crowd. This caused disruption to other trains and placed railway staff and the police themselves at risk. BR's management was understandably concerned, and its chairman, Sir Robert Reid, issued stern instructions that this must not happen again. For the moment, steam was on probation. It was tribute to *Flying Scotsman*'s popularity that so many people wanted to see her – but the irresponsible actions of a few placed main-line steam under a considerable cloud, for a while at least.

Flying Scotsman was allowed to continue operations, and paid a visit to Scotland, where she was adopted by a Territorial Army regiment who placed a guard round her at Eastfield depot. After exhibition at Glasgow Queen Street, she visited Perth and Edinburgh, crossing the Forth Bridge, where she had been so brilliantly captured on canvas by Terence Cuneo.

Flying Scotsman's fame was such that when the Queen Mother opened the North Woolwich Station Museum in London the locomotive hauled the Royal Train. *Flying Scotsman* was burnished to perfection, and when, on the footplate, the Queen Mother was told the locomotive had been built in 1923, she commented wistfully: 'That was the year I was married.' The Royal Train was a huge success, and sealed *Flying Scotsman*'s official approval.

In 1985 *Flying Scotsman* was due for another overhaul to

remain running on the main line. By this time, BR had devised a thorough-going policy to regulate the operation and maintenance of steam locomotives. Once insurance inspectors had confirmed that a locomotive met British Rail's high standards and the boiler was first steamed (even if it had yet to be fitted to the locomotive itself), a clock started ticking. It was given what is known as a boiler certificate to prove it was safe to operate. After ten years, the boiler would have to be removed from the locomotive and completely overhauled, but, in view of the fact that operating at high-speed on the main line was far more demanding than the 25mph maximum allowed on heritage railway, BR stipulated that at the end of seven years on the boiler certificate, it would have to be overhauled and recertified in order to run on the main line – although the owner of the locomotive could, if he or she wanted, use the remaining three years of the boiler certificate on preserved lines if desired.

A key figure was appointed at this time to help keep *Flying Scotsman* running. Roland Kennington was an experienced engineer, and ultimately became engineer-in-charge in 1986. Little could he have suspected just how long he would be involved with *Flying Scotsman* back then! Two days before Christmas 1985, while working at Bedford engineering company WH Allen, he received a phone call from *Flying Scotsman*'s groom, Ray Towell. Part of the valve gear had snapped in two, and, knowing of Kennington's experience with A4 Pacific *Sir Nigel Gresley*, Towell decided to see what WH Allen could do. With the works closed for ten days over Christmas, Kennington said that the best he could do was to weld the part back together. Towell agreed and sent it to Bedford first on a train to Milton Keynes, and thence by taxi. Kennington's work meant that BR allowed *Flying Scotsman* to make two journeys with it, and the special trains planned to mark the fiftieth birthday of *Flying Scotsman*'s owner William McAlpine ran satisfactorily.

Four months later, Kennington was called by the head of SLOA, and the man in operational charge of *Flying Scotsman*, Bernard Staite. He told Kennington that McAlpine wanted to move *Flying Scotsman* from Carnforth and the team that was looking after her. Kennington thinks that the broken part of the valve gear (which had been caused by a bolt left in the motion during the overhaul) was a contributory factor. McAlpine wanted the locomotive cared for by a group of volunteers, with Kennington as honorary chief engineer. After careful consideration, Kennington decided he could fit *Flying Scotsman* in with his day job and family commitments and readily agreed.

From Carnforth, it was decided to move *Flying Scotsman* south to London's Marylebone station, where a number of special steam-hauled trains to Stratford-upon-Avon called 'The Shakespeare Express' were to run. Marylebone was that rare thing: a station with an operational turntable on which the locomotives could turn round easily. London's terminus stations were new ground for main-line steam in the 1980s, and the first locomotive to break it was, appropriately, ex-LNER A4 Pacific No. 4498 *Sir Nigel Gresley*, which had first been unveiled in front of her designer at Marylebone in November 1937.

Flying Scotsman took her turns on the Shakespeare Express, returning to the station to which Ken Issitt and Cyril Chamberlain had nursed her after her almost final journey in the early 1950s. It was a happy reunion, and *Flying Scotsman* proved an extravagantly able performer on the train. She seemed happy in the capital, and in view of new opportunities for main-line running from there, McAlpine leapt at the opportunity to base her at the old Great Western steam shed in Southall, not far from Paddington, in 1987. *Flying Scotsman* now had her own home from home. She would remain there until 2004.

The following year, 1987, was another busy year for *Flying Scotsman*, with charters running mainly in the Midlands and northern England. She returned to Sellafield on a series of regular trains called 'The Sellafield Sightseer' to promote the new visitor centre at the nuclear power station. However, anti-nuclear protestors ensured that, while the trains got plenty of coverage, it wasn't the sort BR wanted. (Sadly, by raising concerns about the safety of the area, the nuclear protestors inadvertently all but killed off main-line steam on the beautiful Cumbrian Coast.) *Flying Scotsman* also ran on the south-western main line west of Basingstoke: another 'new' route for steam which had been cleared by British Rail. Enthusiasts would have to make the most of her, however, because McAlpine soon received an irresistible offer to take *Flying Scotsman* to Australia to mark the country's bicentennial. Mindful of the experience in America, there were plenty of worried people who feared that history would repeat itself.

Chapter Thirteen
Australian Interlude

Nineteen-eighty-eight saw Australia celebrate its bicentennial: 200 years since Governor Phillips landed in what is now known as Botany Bay. The country was going to celebrate in style, and a group of railway enthusiasts decided to organise a 'steam spectacular' which would be held in October in Melbourne, the city where the country's first steam locomotive operated. The Australians, like the British, take their railway heritage seriously, and each state has its own collection of historic rolling stock. The organisers of the steam spectacular wanted representatives from each state, and, to mark the connections with Britain, they also decided to try and get a British locomotive. The easiest thing to do would have been to have hired *Pendennis Castle*, which was then in Australia, from its owner Rio Tinto; failing that, a number of Great Central Railway-designed freight locomotives had been sent to Australia after the First World War, and one of these would also have been a suitable representative. The small committee organising the show decided they wanted something more iconic and famous, though. Its chairman, Melbourne postman Walter Stuchbery, approached the National Railway Museum to see if they would loan the record-holding A4 *Mallard*. The

Museum declined, as it had restored *Mallard* to working order to celebrate the fiftieth anniversary of its historic sprint down Stoke Bank, so *Mallard* was going to stay in Britain. They didn't leave Stuchbery without ideas, though; if *Mallard* was tied up, they might have more success approaching Sir William McAlpine for *Flying Scotsman* instead.

McAlpine was receptive to the idea, but he did have one concern: 'I'd got the organisers to guarantee a return ticket for *Flying Scotsman* – we'd been here before!' he said. Stuchbery mortgaged his house to secure *Flying Scotsman*'s return home, and McAlpine agreed to send her on another epic adventure. Hinchcliffe, who had accompanied *Flying Scotsman* to America, was also positive: 'I think it's a wonderful opportunity,' he bubbled. 'And not only is the engine looking forward to it, so are all the volunteers too.'

But before she could go abroad, she had to have an air-braking system fitted in order to haul trains there as her train brakes worked on the vacuum principle and were incompatible with the air-braked coaches used in Australia. An air compressor was borrowed from the Nene Valley Railway in Cambridgeshire, and the support team, led by Kennington, worked night and day to ensure that the components most likely to fail were in tip-top condition. They even replaced the steel tyres on the driving wheels, as these were wearing thin.

Flying Scotsman departed Britain on the P&O ship *New Zealand Pacific* as deck cargo. Her loading and departure were headline news, but this was definitely 'au revoir' –

McAlpine and Stuchbery had done enough to ensure that there would be no repeats of the American mishaps! On her voyage, she was doused with fresh water daily to protect her paintwork, and as she crossed the Equator was given a ceremonial splashing and a certificate to say she had crossed the Line. She was being treated more like a pampered racehorse than a steam locomotive.

Kennington, who would accompany *Flying Scotsman* throughout the tour, flew out a few days before the ship was due to arrive in Sydney. Plans to unload her in Melbourne foundered when it was discovered the crucial floating crane had been sold, so she was to be unloaded in Sydney instead.

Australian railway officials quizzed Kennington about *Flying Scotsman*. Would she, they asked, be able to climb the five-mile long, 1-in-37 Cowan Bank with a trailing load of 300 tonnes without assistance? What were the brake shoes made of? Were electric lights fitted? Kennington reassured them that *Flying Scotsman* would be able to cope with everything demanded of her, and with that, the officials were satisfied. She was unloaded in sight of Sydney Harbour Bridge with great care and ceremony on 16 October, and after last-minute adjustments, the Australian operating authorities certified her for main-line operation. With that, Kennington and the team wasted no time in giving her a test run. With just three coaches behind her, she ran from Sydney to Port Kembla and back, a distance of 125 miles; everything was in fine fettle, and five days after landing she was able to go to Melbourne.

The organisers planned a night-time departure to enable

her to benefit from the cooler temperatures, and to spend as much time as possible at the steam spectacular. She hauled her tender, a spares van and a water tanker, and her journey wasn't expected to be noticed – but that couldn't have been more wrong. Word spread like wildfire – *Flying Scotsman* was here! Thousands upon thousands lined the tracks to see her go past: the reception was as epic as the setting.

After a settling-in period, *Flying Scotsman* began to earn her keep on passenger trains. Because there were two standard-gauge lines and one 3ft-6in-gauge line in parallel near Melbourne, Stuchbery and the organisers were able to arrange for three steam-hauled trains to run side-by-side. It was 'the most exciting thing' that McAlpine remembered from Australia – an absolutely spectacular sight, and it set the standard for everything that was to follow.

Large crowds were something of a problem, and it was a constant challenge to keep passengers and spectators apart. Sometimes the crew had little option but to open *Flying Scotsman*'s draincocks and send a jet of steam from the cylinders in order to persuade people to get out of the way. On a trip to Albury a broken spring was noticed, quite a serious problem, but a local blacksmith came to the rescue, effecting a temporary repair which allowed *Flying Scotsman* to get back to Melbourne without further incident. *Flying Scotsman* wasn't universally popular with everyone: a hurrying motorist got hit on an unmanned level crossing. It could have been fatal, but what was beyond belief to the train crew was the fact that, after knocking off the left-hand front steps and draincock pipes, the motorist reversed the car, turned round and sped off in a cloud of smoke!

Flying Scotsman stayed in Melbourne for two months before making the 600-mile journey north back to Sydney. More than 130,000 people had paid to see her, and receipts had almost covered the transport costs. In Sydney she was welcomed, appropriately, by a pipe band and (by now to nobody's surprise) a huge crowd of over 5,000 people. During December, she was used on an intensive tour programme, the highlights of which were the times she worked with Australia's flagship Pacific, No. 3801. This beautiful green machine, almost the same colour as *Flying Scotsman*, and every bit as elegant, has a bullet-shaped nose and stream-lined fairings, and the Australians are rightly proud of her. No. 3801 and *Flying Scotsman* were a glamorous pair, and the public adored them.

Kennington and the various volunteers, some from England, some from Australia, spent January maintaining *Flying Scotsman* to keep her in the condition to which she was accustomed. February and March saw her work a number of short-distance tours, though on one memorable occasion, she and No. 3801 worked the 614 miles to Brisbane. She stayed in Sydney until July, and proved a smash-hit down under, carrying thousands, and watched by many thousands more. She then returned to Melbourne briefly to prepare for an epic twenty-eight-day tour north to Alice Springs and then south again to Adelaide.

And it took some preparation: eighty tonnes of coal were bagged up for the trip, and three water tanks were connected first to each other, and then to *Flying Scotsman*'s tender. Seven sold-out coaches carried passengers who had paid top-dollar to witness another spectacular record fall: an attempt was to be made on the non-stop steam record, which stood at 408.6 miles, recorded by A4 Pacifics hauling the 'Flying Scotsman' train in 1948. Operational preparation was critical too. The 422 miles between Parkes and Broken Hill was single-track, and trains could only pass at short sections of double-track called 'loops'. Four trains had to be crossed, and water had to be pumped from the tank wagons to the tender. In the coach behind the tanks waited a crew member with a petrol-driven water pump. On the order, he would start the pump, and some of the 26,000 gallons of water would go into *Flying Scotsman*'s tender.

The run on 8 August 1989 was truly heroic. Even though there were problems with two of the critical token exchanges, without which *Flying Scotsman* would not have been permitted on to sections of single track, and even though a lorry crossed the line just a few feet in front of the train 80 miles short of the destination, *Flying Scotsman* performed like the thoroughbred she was. After nine hours and twenty-five minutes, *Flying Scotsman* arrived at Broken Hill, having consumed just 16,000 gallons of her 25,000-gallon water supply. 'We could have gone much, much further!' beamed a delighted McAlpine, who was on the train at the time.

The final stage of the journey to Alice Springs was memorable for different reasons. The old narrow-gauge line had just been replaced by standard-gauge track, and *Flying Scotsman* would be the first steam locomotive to traverse it:

in fact, she would be the first steam locomotive in Alice Springs for years. The 775-mile line was long enough for a diesel locomotive to be attached to the train in case *Flying Scotsman* failed, but that was never likely with Kennington on the shovel, and the able hand of former Pacific driver David Rollins on the regulator.

This wasn't a non-stop run, and efforts were made to stop at settlements en route to give as many people as possible the chance to see the locomotive. As a result the journey took thirty hours in total, but arrival in Alice Springs was worth the wait. McAlpine, who was on the footplate, was overwhelmed by what he saw: 'When we went there, they closed schools, and people were lining the track for miles. I think the whole town must have turned out!' Of all the welcomes accorded *Flying Scotsman* during her stay in Australia, this was the most spectacular. Aborigines staged a ceremony too, welcoming *Flying Scotsman* formally to their land: it was a unique recognition of her personality and character.

She returned from Alice Springs to Adelaide, but, while the original plan had been to go to Sydney for her journey home, it was now decided she should go to Perth instead. Crossing the world's longest straight bit of railway, 297 miles of arrow-straight track on the Nullarbor Plain, she took five days. During that time, problems with the air compressor meant that a diesel locomotive was needed to assist braking, and the hard water had fractured piston rings in the right-hand cylinder and damaged the valve head, leading to some cautious running.

It was a long, tiring journey, but Western Australia rolled

out the red carpet for *Flying Scotsman*, the public's appetite for this iconic locomotive undimmed by time. Here, something truly amazing had been arranged – something that you'd have got incredible odds from the bookmakers if you'd placed a bet even five years before. *Flying Scotsman* came smokebox-to-smokebox with her old rival, and former stablemate, *Pendennis Castle*. 'That was amazing,' recalls McAlpine, 'because I actually had a painting of the two of them together at Carnforth commissioned, because I never thought I would see them together again. Off *Pendennis* went, and in Australia they met buffer to buffer!' It was an emotional reunion, and for a few blissful weeks, the pair worked special trains, occasionally double-heading. It was a fitting climax to a tour that had succeeded beyond anyone's expectations.

It couldn't last forever, and after spending a short time in Sydney, where she spent a short time running, gaining thirteen minutes on the twenty-four-minute schedule on the notorious Cowan Bank (one of the steepest railway gradients in Australia), *Flying Scotsman* was loaded on the French cargo ship *La Perouse*, heading on the easterly route via Cape Horn to Tilbury. In the process, she became the first locomotive to circumnavigate the globe.

For all involved, the visit to Australia had been a massive success. Stuchbery's dream of seeing *Flying Scotsman* in Melbourne had come true, and thousands (probably hundreds of thousands) of people who might never have dreamed of seeing her in the flesh got their chance. She had run something like 28,000 miles without a critical failure, and she had looked magnificent throughout. From the ecstatic receptions she received, to the unbelievable non-stop run, it had been a fantastic year, and one which will live long in the memories of everyone involved.

Chapter Fourteen
Return

Flying *Scotsman* landed safely back in Britain just before Christmas 1989. Her tour to Australia had been a huge success, and the locomotive was headline news again. On arrival at Southall, Kennington immediately gave her a thorough inspection, but to his delight, found she needed relatively little work to make her fit for service. (Kennington now found himself with much more time on his hands, as he had been made redundant by his employer just two weeks before he returned from Australia. It wasn't a surprise to him, but it must have been a bitter blow to take.)

Her first run back in Britain was on a special train called 'The FSS Executive', which ran from Didcot to Banbury. The managing director of BR's Intercity sector, Dr John Prideaux, unveiled a plaque below her nameplates to commemorate the epic non-stop run between Parkes and Broken Hill. Thankfully for the enthusiasts, there was no further talk of foreign adventures!

Flying Scotsman next found herself temporarily based at Crewe to work trains on the delightful North Wales Coast line to Holyhead. Though it was unfamiliar territory, she performed impeccably, winning new admirers in the Principality she had first visited in 1963. However, on one of the trains, disaster struck when a passenger leaning out of a door window struck his head on the wall of Penmaenbach Tunnel, suffering fatal injuries. Many enthusiasts travelling on rail tours appreciated the drop-down windows on the doors (through which the doors were opened from the inside), as they could lean out and see the locomotive hauling the train. At the time of the accident there was a great deal of soul-searching, but reluctantly, the decision was taken to fit bars to the windows to prevent a repeat of the tragedy.

In September 1990, to mark the twenty-fifth anniversary of the popular Severn Valley Railway in Shropshire, *Flying Scotsman* made a rare visit to a preserved line, and the heritage railway was rewarded with full trains and linesides packed with people taking pictures. 'If you charged £1 for every picture taken,' says a wistful McAlpine, 'you could overhaul her every year!'

Flying Scotsman's condition was still reasonable, but she was rapidly approaching the end of her seven-year main-line boiler certificate. McAlpine, who had long recognised that *Flying Scotsman* was most profitable visiting heritage railways, decided that, rather than undergo another expensive seven-year overhaul, she should go on tour to such railways around the country until her boiler certificate ran out in a couple of years' time.

This was something that hadn't been possible when McAlpine repatriated *Flying Scotsman* in the 1970s. Then there were just a handful of heritage railways, and few were long enough, or had good enough facilities, to handle an engine of her size. The track on many was lightly laid and would have taken a battering too. But in the intervening twenty years, the heritage railway movement had blossomed, and there were now three lines longer than fifteen miles, and a good few approaching ten: long enough for *Flying Scotsman* to stretch her legs.

More crucially, passenger numbers had boomed too. A combination of great marketing, public nostalgia and the influence of Thomas the Tank Engine on the little ones meant that heritage railways were now regarded as key tourist attractions in almost every area they served. Engineering capabilities had also improved in leaps and bounds. Whereas replacing the boiler tubes of a locomotive in the 1970s would have seemed a major task, creative and brilliant engineers had devised ways of keeping the giants of steam running safely for longer than anyone had anticipated. The time was right for *Flying Scotsman* to rejoin this movement.

Heritage railways around the country submitted bids to run *Flying Scotsman*, and she immediately proved a smash hit. When she visited the Birmingham Railway Museum in Tyseley, she was used on 'driver experience' duties, where, for a fee, members of the public could have the opportunity to drive and fire this priceless icon, under close supervision, of course. She then visited the Great Central Railway at Loughborough, and the East Lancashire Railway at Bury before heading back into Wales to visit the Llangollen Railway.

The Llangollen Railway is among the prettiest in Britain, and at six miles long offered a reasonable opportunity for *Flying Scotsman* to stretch her legs. A wide-ranging variety of duties was planned, from ordinary passenger trains, to driver experience courses, to dining trains, all in a bid to give as many people as possible as many ways to experience *Flying Scotsman* as possible. The aim was to raise money for much-needed track and bridge improvements, and *Flying Scotsman* offered a really good way of raising funds.

However, on arrival at Llangollen in March 1993, it became apparent that *Flying Scotsman* was not in good enough health to do any running at all. While she was with the Great Central Railway, a leak from one of the flue tubes in the boiler had been noticed. It started off as a minor leak from the boiler into the tubes the fire passed through, and in all probability sealed up as soon as the boiler got hot and expanded slightly. But, as ever is the case with these things, the problem gradually got worse. By the time *Flying Scotsman* had reached Bury, the tubes required attention every morning before she started in service, and by Llangollen the leak was described, memorably, as being like a waterfall. There was no way she could operate safely. The Llangollen Railway made the best of a bad job by offering footplate visits at £1 a time, so *Flying Scotsman*'s visit wasn't entirely in vain.

There was little point in spending a huge amount of money on *Flying Scotsman*'s boiler, but salvation was at hand when the West Midlands engineering firm of FKI Babcock Robey agreed to retube the boiler at no charge: at their Oldbury worksite wanted the world to know about the quality of its workmanship and the generosity of the company. For the first time since 14 February 1963, she was to appear in public in her last front-line livery, the

Brunswick green of British Railways, after her volunteers asked McAlpine for permission. Conscious of the immense effort and commitment they had given the locomotive, he readily agreed. She was fitted with a double-chimney, given smoke-deflecting plates at the side of the smokebox, and renumbered to 60103. She couldn't have looked more different from the apple green colour she had by now carried for most of her life if she'd wanted to.

Nineteen-ninety-three was a momentous year. After thirty years of outright ownership, McAlpine went into partnership with the music mogul and rail enthusiast Pete Waterman. McAlpine had bought the Pullman train from the SLOA after the boss of Intercity's special trains unit, David Ward, suggested that he bought his own set of carriages to keep them running. It was sound advice because, with privatisation of the railways on the horizon, there was no guarantee these increasingly venerable coaches would receive the same care and attention that Intercity lavished on them. But to McAlpine's horror – and in all likelihood to Ward's surprise – asbestos was found in some of the coaches during overhaul. As the material was now banned, specialist contractors had to be found to remove it safely.

Waterman, meanwhile, had been busy acquiring a number of diesel and steam locomotives in anticipation of privatisation. Waterman wanted to run the first train in privatisation, and had spent a fortune overhauling a heritage diesel to demanding standards in a bid to break the preserved diesel ban that BR had imposed when enthusiasts started to buy surplus locomotives.

By the early 1990s, British Rail was among the most efficient state-owned railways in the world. It had finally found the holy grail of organisation which had proved so elusive since 1923 – rather than organising things on a regional basis, the railway was managed based on the type of traffic. This meant that commuter trains around London were in one part of the organisation, and freight in another; Scotland's services were in a separate company; long-distance express services were run by InterCity (a massive success story in its own right); and local and regional services everywhere else were operated by the Regional Railways division. Even after all the privatisations of the 1980s, Margaret Thatcher found herself acknowledging that BR was working well, and that to privatise it would be like selling the family silver.

However, John Major's government, which succeeded Thatcher's, disagreed. The railway would be sold and split up so comprehensively that renationalisation would be difficult if not impossible. The plan was to have one company owning the tracks, which would be floated on the stock market. The rail freight companies were to be sold off in their entirety too, but passenger trains were to be run on a franchised basis. Traffic was split up first by type, and then by region, so that there were more than twenty companies operating passenger trains. Furthermore – and this was why Waterman wanted to run trains – any company that wanted to do so could (providing it met certain financial and safety criteria) run trains on the network: something known as 'open access'. This meant Waterman could run charter trains in his own right, without depending on another company to provide locomotives, carriages and staff. Privatisation was too tempting for him to resist.

Waterman had been an apprentice in the 1960s at the former Great Western locomotive works in Stafford Road, Wolverhampton, before embarking on a highly successful career in showbiz that included launching the careers of Kylie Minogue and Jason Donovan, among others. He had seen the reaction of visitors to the East Lancashire Railway. As he told *The Railway Magazine* editor Nick Piggott:

> I must say that LNER locomotives don't do a lot for me. I'm a Great Western and LNWR enthusiast, and I wouldn't normally go out of my way to see the A3 working, but on that occasion I thought I'd pop up to Bury because of my contacts with Bill.
>
> The old girl was in a hell of a state mechanically, but the one thing I couldn't get over was the adulation – people were even buying lumps of coal off her!

Waterman rang McAlpine, and after a meeting in May 1993 the pair agreed to go into partnership.

Though McAlpine acknowledges that sharing the financial burden of running *Flying Scotsman* was part of his motivation, he was also concerned about the future. 'I am not immortal, and if I had died without making plans, *Flying Scotsman* could possibly have ended up in a situation that would not have been in her best interests,' he said at the time. 'Now, Pete is a little younger than I, and I now feel that the locomotive's future is secure.' The sentiment is typical of the man – while retaining his sound business sense, he was also looking ahead, and felt strongly that *Flying Scotsman* should stay running rather than being a stuffed-and-mounted exhibit at a museum.

Released to traffic in 1993 in the guise of her final, most powerful form, *Flying Scotsman* went back on tour of the preserved lines. First was the Paignton & Dartmouth Steam Railway (the current name of the Torbay Railway, which she had visited thirty years before), then to the Gloucestershire and Warwickshire Railway, the Nene Valley Railway in Peterborough, and the Swanage and Severn Valley Railways, before visiting the Birmingham Railway Museum again. Finally, in the spring of 1995, in the last year of her boiler certificate, she reached the Llangollen Railway, where it was hoped she would repay her debt of honour to the dedicated volunteers there.

She came agonisingly close to doing so, but then suffered what engineers call an 'all-wheels' derailment at low speed. While one set of wheels can usually be jacked back on to the rails, this was rather trickier to recover, and specialist lifting gear had to be called out from Crewe. Once on the rails, a crack in the firebox soon became apparent. This was worse than a leaking tube, and the insurance inspector sent to see if the boiler was safe soon gave McAlpine and Waterman his verdict: 'If it was a horse, I'd have it shot,' he said.

There was no option: *Flying Scotsman* had to come back to Southall for overhaul, but McAlpine and Waterman could spare neither the time nor the money to give *Flying Scotsman* top priority, because their partnership business was becoming increasingly time-consuming as the complexities of privatisation became all-too-apparent. Funds became tight, and *Flying Scotsman* was mortgaged to secure the future of their joint venture.

By March 1996 Waterman revealed to the press that he was 'totally fed up' with the privatisation process. His ambitions to make money from the privatised railway were thwarted, and he offered his surplus locomotives for sale. The fact that it took longer than expected to remove the asbestos from the former SLOA Pullman coaches McAlpine had acquired also deprived the partnership of a potentially lucrative revenue stream for a whole season. Too much happened in too short a time, and Waterman decided to curtail his active involvement in the rail industry, though his Waterman Railways company eventually refocused on engineering, rebranded itself as LNWR, and continues to operate from Crewe. The partnership between Waterman and McAlpine never went bust, despite popular myth, and, while *Flying Scotsman* was unlikely to steam in the near future, at least she was safe.

Chapter Fifteen
The Marchington Years

I n 1996 *Flying Scotsman* faced an uncertain operational future. Neither Pete Waterman nor William McAlpine were keen to spend yet more money on an expensive overhaul, and, now out of traffic and with no revenue stream, it looked like it was going to be a while before she would steam again. Waterman and McAlpine were busy trying to make a success of the former British Rail special trains unit, which was sold at privatisation: as McAlpine says, *Flying Scotsman had* to take a back seat: 'There was no point in overhauling *Scotsman* when you couldn't make it pay on the main line.'

McAlpine wanted to do a less expensive overhaul that would allow *Flying Scotsman* to run on preserved lines, but there were many who felt that limiting this icon to just 25mph was rather like caging a lion. It was main line or nothing, felt its supporters. 'Keeping an engine in captivity running at 25mph isn't as exciting as main-line running,' said McAlpine, 'but it is profitable!' Then, in an interview, Waterman casually mentioned that *Flying Scotsman* was worth around £1.3 million. He didn't say he and McAlpine wanted to sell her: they didn't — but that was the inference many drew. It didn't take long for a buyer to make an approach.

The man in question was a successful businessman, long-time steam enthusiast and self-confessed traction engine 'nut', Dr Tony Marchington. Marchington had just floated his biotechnology company Oxford Molecular on the stock market, and by all accounts had £5 million burning a hole in his pocket.

His interest in steam traction had developed from his upbringing. He hailed from the Buxton area of Derbyshire and had grown up with farm machinery. With his father he had built up a substantial collection of steam traction engines and fairground rides that became a great passion for him, and it was this passion that inexorably drew him towards *Flying Scotsman*. He didn't simply want *Flying Scotsman* because it was a steam engine and he fancied having a go, as a trophy – he was passionate about the locomotive and wanted to see it run on the main line.

Marchington wasted no time in getting in touch with McAlpine. The two had met before, when Marchington had visited McAlpine's traction engine collection and asked to see it; McAlpine, on his way out in a dinner jacket and black tie, said: 'Well, here's the key. Just put them back when you've finished.' Marchington wanted to spend £1.3 million on the locomotive, and another £300,000 or so overhauling her for main-line operation. 'It was a sensible thing,' says McAlpine. 'We were running the special trains unit which was a growing business and just didn't have the time to devote to her.'

So Marchington acquired *Flying Scotsman* from McAlpine and Waterman and started to formulate his plans to make her pay. (A year later he added to his collection by buying one of *Flying Scotsman*'s cousins, A4 60019 *Bittern* – another locomotive in need of a major restoration before it could work again.) Despite what some have said since, this wasn't a purchase made on a whim. Marchington had formulated a daring, but apparently sensible business plan which would see *Flying Scotsman* and *Bittern* hauling a series of £250-per-head dining trains from the London area. It would be a glamorous operation, using original Pullman cars and spoiling passengers with the last word in luxury. There was even the possibility of running a £2,000-per-head millennium-eve train from London to Edinburgh using *Flying Scotsman*. This was, and would prove, a cogent vision. Whatever the external events that would follow, back in 1997 there's no doubt that Marchington's plan looked like the best sort of deal *Flying Scotsman* was going to get.

But what Marchington hadn't realised – though McAlpine had recognised it back in the 1970s – was just how hard making money with a 1923-built steam locomotive in the 1990s was going to be. Leaving aside the commercial considerations, the engineering and operational challenges would have stumped many: it speaks volumes for Marchington's tenacity that he was able to get her running at all.

When he bought *Flying Scotsman* she had been out of traffic for three years or so, stored at Crewe awaiting her next full ten-yearly overhaul, after failing with boiler troubles at the Llangollen Railway close to the end of her previous ten-year boiler certificate for both main-line and preserved railway work. Marchington had budgeted an overhaul cost of around £300,000: in line with that of other similar-sized engines that had needed similar work. Nobody – not Marchington, McAlpine, Waterman or *Flying Scotsman*'s dedicated supporters – could have expected the ferocious cost of bringing 'Scotsman' back to life. Over the first three years of ownership Marchington spent a gigantic £750,000 rebuilding the engine to operational standards, billed as the most expensive steam locomotive overhaul in the fifty-five-year history of the steam preservation movement. Many had suggested *Flying Scotsman* was jinxed and had some kind of curse, because it caused so much trouble for Alan Pegler in America, and the spiralling cost of the 1996–1999 overhaul did nothing to undermine this school of thought. But the truth is rather different. Rebuilding a locomotive like *Flying Scotsman* is always going to be hugely expensive, especially when you consider that fireboxes like hers are prone to potentially dangerous cracking that demands sophisticated repairs in any case.

During the overhaul, Marchington wasn't able to earn a penny back, as the locomotive was stripped down to her component parts for the rebuild, and eventually further finance had to be sought to continue with the project. He went to the banks: a reasonable short-term decision given the credibility of his business case. The loan was secured against the engine, which may seem like a risky idea, but it wasn't unheard of. Preserved railways have in the past secured loans against locomotives – even if it hasn't been revealed publicly – as, if the worst happens and the line runs out of money, it's better to lose one of many locomotives rather than have the bank come in and take away the whole train set. The difference with *Flying Scotsman* was that she would be Marchington's only revenue stream.

Operating a steam locomotive is now, as Marchington found, a cripplingly expensive business, and *Flying Scotsman*'s overhaul wasn't the first or the last to spiral way beyond initial forecasts. For steam locomotives the world has changed massively since BR steam came to an end in 1968. Back in the 1950s – and even in the early 1960s – new components were available off the shelf at major works like Doncaster on the Eastern Region and Swindon on the Western Region. Boilers were built new, and rarely was there an economic case for rebuilding a boiler after years of use. It was always deemed better to select a new part and put each locomotive back in traffic in the very best possible condition in the shortest time possible.

In fact, Swindon Works, the former hub of the Great Western Railway, was a prime example of mass production. Many of the locomotive classes in service used common parts, be it boilers, wheels or just cab components, and that contributed to making the cost of running a fleet of locomotives much cheaper than it is today to keep one example in traffic. Today *Flying Scotsman*'s boiler is around forty-five years old. If it had been in traffic with the other seventy-eight Gresley A3s, new boilers or boiler exchanges would have been possible and regular. When an engine came into works while in service with the LNER and BR it was always a requirement that repairs should be undertaken quickly and efficiently, and that was made possible by a vast number of spares being available at all times.

For preserved steam locomotives the world couldn't be more different or harder. If something breaks, there simply isn't a spare part sitting on the shelf at the local 'Kwik Fit', waiting to be bolted on. That part has to be repaired or made from scratch by skilled men who have the 'know-how' to machine, weld, fabricate and fit a myriad of parts from boiler tubes to regulator glands and motion components. Few locomotive overhauls have cost as much as the 1996–1999 rebuild of *Flying Scotsman*, but big engines require big sums of money to be invested just to keep them in working order – ask any of the other operators of large 'Pacifics', like Brell Ewart of the Princess Royal Class Locomotive Trust, and they will tell you the same.

Of course, *Flying Scotsman* is special, but the cost of overhauling the national icon is in the same league as other large Pacifics, such as the erstwhile *Duchess of Sutherland*, *Clan Line* and *Sir Nigel Gresley*. All of these giants of steam are big Pacifics weighing in at more than 150 tonnes, with driving wheels that tower above the rails to heights of 6ft 8in, boilers pressurised to over 200lbs/sq in. and giant fireboxes that burn coal like it's going out of fashion – and they all need professional skilled engineers to keep them running, and a lot of money and time.

The youngest preserved steam locomotives being restored now are at least forty-six years-old – the BR 'Standard' designs built between 1951 and 1960 and they are still thought of as 'modern engines' by many steam men. In the case of *Flying Scotsman* the owners are responsible for an eighty-three-year-old racehorse which has had extensive surgery over the years, with new parts, improvements to the design and thousands upon thousands of miles in service. In fact National Railway Museum Head of Knowledge and Collections Helen Ashby believes there are now no original mechanical components left on *Flying Scotsman*.

All this takes its toll and in the twenty-first century preservation is taking on some of the most ambitious and challenging restoration projects in the history of the steam movement – including locomotives that were once thought to be way beyond repair – and it is now not so much a question of 'Can it be done?', but of 'How can it be done?' and 'How much?' Today the average overhaul costs between £100,000 for an average tank engine to £300,000 for a middle-sized, mixed-traffic locomotive. One can hardly blame Marchington for being surprised when *Flying Scotsman*'s overhaul cost £750,000 to return to working order in 1999.

The simple truth was that over the previous twenty or so years, *Flying Scotsman* had been worked hard. Operating up to fifty trains per year, with each train covering on average between 200 and 250 miles per trip equates to roughly 10,000 miles per year. How many eighty-three-year-old cars do that sort of mileage? Of course, it's a much lower mileage than she would have recorded in daily service back in the 1950s, but steam was withdrawn almost forty years ago – and *Flying Scotsman*'s career came to an end because she had been in service for four decades then, and covered more than 1.5 million miles in service, the equivalent of travelling to the moon and back three times. It is a tribute to the engineering quality of the 1920s Doncaster Works that sees *Flying Scotsman* still standing before us. If the build quality hadn't been up to scratch, she simply wouldn't be here.

Money has to come from somewhere, and the Heritage Lottery Fund has assisted in the restoration of many steam locomotives, but not all projects can benefit from grant funding, and that included *Flying Scotsman* when she was privately owned. Many locomotives are owned by charities and trusts which rely on the donations of dedicated supporters for most of their funding. *Flying Scotsman* was overhauled and returned to steam using the finances of one man.

Advances in repair techniques have made it possible to repair or replace just about every single component: whether it is a simple cork for an oil pot or a section of boiler barrel, it can be done. The specialist engineering involved in repairing a steam boiler comes at a price, and it has to be done right first time as the boiler and the running gear are highly specialised and safety-critical pieces of precision engineering. A boiler is full of water which is then heated to boiling point by a fire burning at around 2,500°F (contained within the firebox at the back of the boiler). This is what produces steam to move the locomotive – by heating the water in the water space between the walls of the inner firebox and outer wrapper and by hot gases passing through the boiler tubes to heat the water in the boiler barrel. In the case of *Flying Scotsman* the boiler has a maximum working pressure of 220psi, and the metal of the boiler barrel and firebox has to be kept in the best possible condition to avoid the sort of catastrophe that almost befell driver Chamberlain and fireman Issitt in the 1950s.

Add to this detailed examination of around 3,000 stays – lengths of metal that are wound into the outer wrapper (the outside skin of the firebox) and the firebox to create a water space for heating the water to produce steam – and bit by bit you start seeing where the money goes when boilers are overhauled. All this metalwork has to be in excellent condition: a boiler explosion would be immediately fatal for engine crew and others, as well as for the preservation movement as a whole.

The average boiler overhaul for a main-line-registered locomotive now attracts a premium of around £150,000–£300,000 depending on the nature of the work required – some cost more, some cost less, but until engineers begin stripping out the internal components and analysing the metal no one really knows what repairs will be necessary. One of the reasons that the cost is so high is the small number of established contractors available to carry out critical repairs of such precision. Boilers aren't small or easy to move or easy to work on, and they have to be right first time – no question.

Tyres are another expensive commodity, and also difficult to come by. The tyres are the outer rim of the wheel, similar to a car tyre, but in the case of a railway locomotive they are made of steel and have to be heated and cooled to fit the wheels. Only certain factories produce steel tyres to the dimensions required for a locomotive like *Flying Scotsman*, and when they have to be replaced it is an expensive business. The average set of tyres for your car costs £200 for four, whilst to retyre just the six driving wheels of a large 'Pacific' like *Flying Scotsman* would cost tens of thousands of pounds.

So, just the wheels and the boiler are expensive items to fix, and that's before turning to the cylinders and associated motion which convert the steam from the boiler into useable power to move not just the locomotive but heavy trains of up to 500 or more tons. The forces and stresses on the motion are immense, as the pistons and valves that move quickly back and forth inside the cylinders in turn move the connecting and coupling rods – lengths of metal that again transfer the steam power into movement. All these parts have bearings and surfaces that have to be machined to exacting tolerances to ensure that the mechanics of movement keep working every time the engine raises steam and sets out on a journey.

So, *Flying Scotsman*'s overhaul was a complex, awkward and expensive affair that still stands as the most expensive ever. The operation was managed by Roland Kennington, with the locomotive's frames and tender remaining at Southall, West London, for volunteer overhaul, whilst the boiler was sent to Chatham Steam Restorations for a thorough check-over and repair.

It may have cost a fortune, but when the physically

complete 4472 *Flying Scotsman* was unveiled to the public on 28 May 1999 at the former Great Western Railway shed of Southall, West London, few doubted it was money well spent. Marchington's patience and deep pockets were rewarded with one of the most beautiful restoration jobs ever managed. This was the first time Marchington had seen *Flying Scotsman* complete and in steam since he bought her three years before: 'More than anything, I have a tremendous sense of relief. After all the trials and tribulations, it is magnificent to see it all put back together.'

Two months after her public debut, *Flying Scotsman* was back on home turf, standing at London King's Cross station – the starting point for the 'The Flying Scotsman' to Edinburgh since the 1920s – waiting to haul her first mainline special since the early 1990s. Then she had been owned by McAlpine and Waterman. This train, the first under Marchington's ownership, was a sell-out £350-per-head return trip to York, and it was just the start of what appeared to be a promising time for *Flying Scotsman* and Dr Marchington's business Oxford Molecular, which was now in its tenth year selling computer programmes to drug companies.

Her return to steam came at ground-breaking time for main-line steam operations. Just five years earlier the first steam-hauled departure from London Kings Cross for many years had taken place, hauled by *Flying Scotsman*'s cousin, the streamlined A4 60009 *Union of South Africa*. It was a toe in the water, with the train running to Peterborough, but it opened the doors to steam on the East Coast Main Line,

Flying Scotsman's former stamping ground. This line was where Marchington wanted to run his premium dining trains. They would capture the London market and offer real steam haulage by *Flying Scotsman* on its original route: another part of his business plan that made perfect sense commercially, and for those with a sense of history.

Initially, the main-line turns for *Scotsman* loaded well, and it looked as if Marchington's plan was going to justify the faith he'd shown in funding the overhaul. But in October 2000, *Flying Scotsman*'s world fell apart, as Britain's entire railway network went into meltdown following a derailment caused by a broken rail at Hatfield, which killed four people.

Unable to confirm that similar rails all around the country were safe, draconian speed restrictions of 20mph were imposed across the network. Ordinary service trains took hours longer than before to reach their destinations, and for *Flying Scotsman* and other steam locomotives, there was no way they could continue operating on the main line. At a stroke, much of *Flying Scotsman*'s cash flow dried up. Marchington reluctantly decided to sell the Pullman coaches and *Bittern* in order to try and keep alive the possibility that *Flying Scotsman* could continue running.

Not long after *Flying Scotsman* returned to steam the first proposals for a Flying Scotsman village were revealed. Marchington had a good relationship with Peak Rail – a preserved railway which had aspirations to rebuild and reopen the entire Matlock–Buxton line with connections to the national network at both ends. This was ideal, as Marchington was thinking of a steam centre at Ambergate where *Flying Scotsman* would also be based to work along the reopened section of the Matlock–Buxton line and be available for main-line work. It would have been superb: one of the most beautiful engines ever to take to the rails working on one of the most scenic lost railways – ironically, it would have been rather similar to McAlpine's plans for the engine in the mid-1990s. However, reinstating the Matlock to Buxton route would prove too ambitious for Peak Rail, at least on the sort of timescale Marchington had in mind, and Ambergate was, in truth, too far from London for *Flying Scotsman* to be easily able to tap in to the premium dining trains' biggest market.

With little other revenue, a lucrative contract was needed to keep *Flying Scotsman* in service, and that was achieved in 2001, when Marchington landed a five-year deal to haul around fifty luxury dining trains per year for the British part of the Venice Simplon Orient Express company (VSOE). It was a marvellous deal, both for VSOE and *Flying Scotsman*. That contract became *Flying Scotsman*'s main source of income, as the engine was given a monopoly for the luxury trains that would see it paid very well for each job.

Flying Scotsman had a good chance to pay its way with the VSOE contract, hauling premium-fare dining trains from London to destinations in the south. In return, VSOE got a fast, powerful steam locomotive at the very top of her form, and the priceless prestige for its passengers of being hauled by the *Flying Scotsman* herself. *Flying Scotsman* had at this time a better chance than virtually any other preserved steam locomotive in the UK of earning her keep for the long-term.

In 2001 Marchington handed over *Flying Scotsman* to a new company which would own and operate it, Flying Scotsman Plc. This allowed Marchington to continue his involvement with the locomotive whilst other people were paid to manage the locomotive's day-to-day business. Peter Butler was appointed as Chief Executive of Flying Scotsman Plc, and his job related to the commercial operation of the engine. On the ground Roland Kennington was paid expenses to manage the overhaul and future maintenance, whilst former BR Special Trains Manager David Ward later joined the team as Operations Manager.

In 2002 VSOE was paying £5,000 per train for the use of *Flying Scotsman*, and she was booked to haul sixty-eight of its trains that year – a very respectable amount of work, representing earnings of over £300,000 if she hauled every train she was booked for. This put *Flying Scotsman* in a unique position amongst preserved, main-line-certified steam locomotives, because the majority of owners relied on one-off enthusiast charters to draw big sums of money on an occasional basis, along with the goodwill of the many supporters who donated cash towards the continued operation of their particular favourite. Few other locomotives have attracted such lucrative work, the only comparable examples being the hard-working LNER B1 61264 and K1 62005, which have both enjoyed five seasons of regular work together hauling tourist trains along the 42-mile line between Fort William and Mallaig in western Scotland, and former VSOE Pullman stalwart SR 'Merchant Navy' 35028 *Clan Line*.

However, Tony Marchington wasn't serious only about owning *Flying Scotsman*; there was also his other passion, for traction engines, and this was ultimately, but unintentionally, to place a national icon in jeopardy. The battles began when he chose to send *Flying Scotsman* to the Derbyshire Steam Fair in the Peak District in June 2002 to stand on a 100ft length of track. Rather than doing this on a day when the engine wasn't booked for main-line duties with VSOE, he decided to take it away from the £5,000-per-day VSOE work and send it to the rally instead – for free. This caused trouble not just with its main contractor VSOE, but also within the volunteer engineering team which kept the engine running. In fact, so strong was the tension that the volunteer team refused to accompany *Flying Scotsman* to the rally.

The rally caused her to miss not one train, but two. It was held on 1–3 June, and *Flying Scotsman* had VSOE duties on 31 May and 12 June. The first date was cancelled in order to move the locomotive by road to Derbyshire, and then after the event it turned out that there was not enough time before 12 June to thoroughly inspect and recertify the engine after her road journey, as she had to be reweighed and certified before being permitted to run on the national network. So she missed another booked turn.

VSOE of course still ran its dining trains from London on these two dates, but instead the fees went to another Gresley-designed engine, *Union of South Africa*, which was made available to take *Flying Scotsman*'s place at the head of the Pullman stock. Whilst VSOE was upbeat about the opportunity to operate different prestigious locomotives at the head of its luxury dining trains as a positive move for its passengers, who would then be guaranteed steam haulage, they were less than satisfied that *Flying Scotsman* might not be available again on 12 June. VSOE General Manager Bob Barnes was reported as saying, 'If it doesn't appear, it's just another factor that will colour the way things are going.'

By this time *Flying Scotsman* was owned by Flying Scotsman Plc and, according to gossip at the time, the revenue she earned was becoming more and more used to pay director's salaries, rather than (more importantly and logically) to pay her own engineering bills and to service a substantial loan that Marchington had secured against the locomotive.

Things weren't looking good for the Plc, but a rescue plan was devised that would see shares in Flying Scotsman Plc floated on the stock market to raise funds to help pay her debts and keep the locomotive running. There was a positive chance the flotation would raise £2.2 million towards the locomotive's upkeep, the creation of the proposed Flying Scotsman Village (an exhibition centre, which changed location several times before the Plc settled on Edinburgh) and a reduction in the debts secured against her. The target was to sell £800,000-worth of shares in blocks of 675 by 12 January 2002, with the final deadline for share sales coming just thirteen days later on 25 January with the aim of raising the £2.2-million target. In December 2001 Flying Scotsman Plc spokesman Geoff Courteney told the railway press: 'The share scheme seems to be going well,' and added: 'We have had a massive number of requests for prospectuses, but it is impossible to tell how many of these will turn into genuine interest. There is every reason to believe at this stage that the scheme will be a tremendous success.'

The directors of Flying Scotsman Plc were keen to make a profit from one of the greatest names in railway history, and even went as far as to say so in the press as the shares were floated. Chief Executive Peter Butler commented: 'Today marks the beginning of a new chapter for the company and enables us to capitalise on the huge potential of the *Flying Scotsman* brand – probably one of the best-known unexploited brand names in the world.' And the share issue certainly captured the imagination of the media and received a great deal of publicity. But not all was as it appeared in the press, for, whilst it appeared that buyers were purchasing shares in *Flying Scotsman*, they were actually buying shares in the company – a very different beast.

Success would prove elusive for the newly floated company. The first signs that all was not well came in January 2002, when the deadline for share sales came and went without the shares selling out. Inevitably, the deadline was extended, but the share issue still didn't come up to expectations. In total £850,000-worth of shares were sold – less than half of the target of £2.2-million shares – but, on the positive side, their value rose from 38p to 43.5p each on the first day of trading. At least 1,000 railway enthusiasts are known to have purchased shares in the company, each one wanting to own a slice of the prestigious locomotive, even though they were buying shares in the Plc.

The Flying Scotsman Village was a popular talking point for the Plc, which bandied about incredible prospective figures – including a forecast that the 25,000sq-ft village would attract 350,000 visitors in 2003 – but the plans were never received by Edinburgh Council. Such visitor numbers were greater than Britain's biggest pay-to-ride railway attraction, the North Yorkshire Moors Railway, and second only to the UK's most popular museum outside London, the National Railway Museum itself. And, despite the hype about visitors and the impressive-sounding size of the Edinburgh village, it was never explained how the Plc would operate the locomotive on London-based trains on a regular basis whilst still attracting visitors to Edinburgh to see nothing of the famous engine. Even if it had been on display, it wouldn't have been as impressive as seeing the engine in steam on the main line. The flaws in the plan were glaring, the targets ambitious, to put it charitably, and by now the business plan was unclear.

For three years Flying Scotsman Plc traded a loss. In 2001 it lost £360,000, and the next year £555,929. Still, the Edinburgh-based Flying Scotsman Village was the golden goose that would turn the books around, with forecast earnings of £988,000 for the Plc in 2003, followed by a surplus of £2.75 million in 2004. None of that happened, and the year end came and went without any physical progress on the Edinburgh Village project.

Marchington had already placed himself in the firing line once when he transferred ownership of *Flying Scotsman* to Flying Scotsman Plc while he retained the original and valuable nameplates. Then in 2002 the revelation hit the streets that he was planning to sell both original nameplates from *Flying Scotsman*. This caused uproar in the steam movement.

Britain's biggest railwayana auction house, Sheffield Railwayana, was offered the opportunity to sell the nameplates for £50,000 each, but declined on the grounds that the asking price was too high, and because, according to the railway press, Sheffield Railwayana boss Ian Wright said it was like 'selling the family silver'. But that didn't stop Marchington continuing to try and sell these most famous of nameplates elsewhere: later in 2002, at an auction in Derbyshire held by Smith Hodgkinson, they were listed again. Despite a bid of £55,000 they weren't sold, although many items from Dr Marchington's private traction engine collection were sold, raising £700,000. It must have been heartbreaking for him, but he must have felt he had little choice: it's pretty clear that by now Marchington was running out of cash. The high hopes of the late 1990s seemed to have been dashed, and the collapse of Dr Marchington's main business Oxford Molecular in the dot.com crash of the early twenty-first century was just another nail in the coffin.

December 2002 was a bad time for *Flying Scotsman* and the Plc. Positive publicity started the final month of the year, when *Flying Scotsman* achieved a new preservation record by hauling a 600-ton train unaided up the 1-in-46 incline of Rattery Bank in Devon, and later in the month plans leaked to the press that *Flying Scotsman*'s Chief Engineer Roland Kennington was in discussions about running a commemorative non-stop train from London to Edinburgh to mark the seventy-fifth anniversary of her epic run in 1928.

Soon after that announcement, Flying Scotsman Plc decided to sell the second tender it had been hoped would give the locomotive crucial extra range (it was three years behind schedule, due to a lack of money to invest in the project). The second tender was crucial to Kennington's idea for a non-stop run as, in fact, the locomotive would need three tenders – where the third would come from was unclear – to provide enough water for the full journey of 393 miles. An agreement was reached for the Plc to hire the tender from new owner Jeremy Hosking, the man who two years earlier had bought A4 60019 *Bittern* from Marchington. It would have been an amazing event that might just have turned things around for Flying Scotsman Plc, but, unknown to the company, it was about to be dealt a near-lethal blow.

VSOE, the company that had provided *Flying Scotsman* with such a substantial income, gave the contract to haul its luxury train in the north of England, the Northern Belle, to the Princess Royal Class Locomotive Trust which operates Stanier 'Duchess' 6233 *Duchess of Sutherland*. This was a big problem for the Plc, as the consequent estimated £65,000 per year loss in earnings represented a fifth of the locomotive's annual income. It would also see *Flying Scotsman* haul twenty-nine fewer trains with the loss of the north of England contract. Even worse, *Flying Scotsman*'s duties on the VSOE's trains from London which now formed almost all its work were cut by seven to just thirty-two trains for 2003.

Few comments were made by VSOE management, but it's not hard to suspect that the engine's 'no-show' while it was in Derbyshire must have contributed heavily towards a huge change of heart. While the opportunity to provide variety on the luxury dining trains was a good thing, in practice, *Flying Scotsman* had an aura of prestige and glamour that the substitutes, however capable, simply lacked.

Flying Scotsman operations manager David Ward took a different view of the situation, though. He was conscious that the volunteer engineering team which tended to *Flying Scotsman*'s needs was in danger of being overstretched with the huge number of VSOE duties. While cutting the number of trains would lose revenue for the company, it would give the hard-pressed volunteers more time to prepare and maintain the locomotive to the high standards demanded by the main line without running themselves ragged.

At the end of 2002 and start of 2003, *Flying Scotsman* received more bad news, when its intermediate overhaul overran by sixteen weeks. Just seven weeks had been allocated for the 'Pacific' to be out of traffic, but in the event the total was twenty-three. The overhaul centred on the boiler, and the main body of the work involved replacing thirty small boiler tubes and twelve of the forty-three flue tubes that contain the superheater elements. This would require the superheater elements to be removed and the superheater header too. It was routine, but challenging, maintenance: *Flying Scotsman* and her team simply fell victim to the unexpected glitches that accompany every project. It was plain bad luck, but it couldn't have come at a much worse time.

If everything had gone according to plan *Flying Scotsman*

would have been back out on the main line at the head of a VSOE special from London on 15 February. With the show-stopping engine not available, VSOE turned, once again, to *Union of South Africa*, and, with the overhaul overrunning by so long, *Union of South Africa* was called upon twice more before *Flying Scotsman* was able to return to the main line. Now, the Plc was saddled simultaneously with an undisclosed bill for its overhaul and the loss of a substantial portion of the year's earnings from its lucrative contract.

By now VSOE must have felt that it couldn't risk relying on *Flying Scotsman* alone, because it decided to take a strong line with Flying Scotsman Plc. It took away the exclusive rights for *Flying Scotsman* to haul the London-based trains; so now it was fair game for anyone with a big engine to bid for a slice of this lucrative pie. This was yet another nail in the coffin for the Plc, as the work allocated initially to *Flying Scotsman* could have amounted to fifty trains – or in round figures approximately £250,000.

Seven years after spending £1.3 million to buy the most famous and highly regarded railway locomotive ever built and a month after *Flying Scotsman* finally returned to the rails in June 2003, Dr Marchington resigned from Flying Scotsman Plc, though he retained a shareholding. At the time Plc's spokesman Geoff Courtenay said: 'There is absolutely no possibility that Tony's departure will lead to changes in the locomotive's current programme. He has no day-to-day influence on the company.' And Chief Executive Peter Butler was reported as saying: 'Having rescued 4472 and restored her to main-line condition, Dr Marchington felt it was time to move on. He will be remembered as playing a vital part in the engine's history . . . its appearance on the main line is now largely due to his vision and commitment.'

Butler was right. Marchington's deep pockets and passionate enthusiasm had kept a national icon running and available, at a price, for the public to ride behind. He had funded a comprehensive and beautifully completed overhaul, and he had fought tooth and nail to keep her on the main line. It was the right time to step out of the limelight.

Marchington had the largest single shareholding in Flying Scotsman Plc, but not the overall majority. When he quit the Plc Marchington was listed as being involved in eleven companies at senior level: six active, two in liquidation and three closed. He'd been a man with a vision, with two high-profile steam locomotives (Flying *Scotsman* and A4 *Bittern*) and his own rake of coaches. *Flying Scotsman* had ripped every pound from his pocket, and possibly more, to keep her in running order.

Now, she continued her weekly operations solely under the jurisdiction of the Plc, with no input whatsoever from the man who had bought her in 1996. But at this point the Plc was solely reliant on the VSOE contract to bring in any cash at all. Its eggs were resting perilously in one basket, because the Flying Scotsman Village, promised for 2003, was still nowhere to be seen halfway through the year that it was due to open.

Ironically, given all the turmoil around her, a happy moment in 2003 for *Flying Scotsman* was her appearance at the fabulous Doncaster Works 150th anniversary event held in July that year. For this she received a brand new coat of LNER apple green at the cost of Wabtec, Doncaster Works' new owner, and was back where she had been built in 1923. Better still, the event brought together what will be remembered as the greatest preservation gathering of ex-LNER locomotives of all shapes and sizes, from the magnificent Stirling 'Single' to the world's fastest steam locomotive, Gresley's sublime A4 4468 *Mallard*. There were 31,000 visitors, and *Flying Scotsman* was the number one attraction. It was the people's chance to get close to the people's engine, and the people made full use of it.

That joy was short-lived. The triumph of the event soon paled into insignificance as, just two months later, much more serious issues raised their heads. Marchington declared himself bankrupt, after shares in Oxford Molecular plummeted on the stock market and the company failed. So *Flying Scotsman*'s owner had no money; the plc which had custody of her had no money; and there was nothing set aside for the next £300,000–£500,000 overhaul. Storm clouds were forming; questions like 'Is Scotsman doomed?' hit the headlines of the railway press, and questions about who would pay to keep the engine running soon followed. This was *Flying Scotsman*'s darkest hour since being stranded in the United States in the 1970s. Even her final years in traffic as a work-worn and easily overlooked locomotive in the 1960s didn't compare. The locomotive had led a safe life in preservation since 1973, but now her future was bleak.

Flying Scotsman continued to run on the main line through 2003, but with debts continuing to rise. The loan taken out by Marchington and secured against the locomotive had been transferred to the Plc with the engine in 2001, and in 2003 the interest alone is believed to have required over £200,000. Money troubles didn't end there. Directors' salaries were being paid from *Flying Scotsman* earnings, and the losses were beginning to snowball. In 2002 the Plc made a loss of £474,619 on earnings of just £238,102, and the shares were doing poorly on the stock market, dipping from a high of 43.5p each to just 30.5p. Then grave news came on 22 October when it was revealed at the Flying Scotsman Plc annual general meeting that the company would be out of money in nine months' time. Auctioneers had been lined up to sell the locomotive if repayments to the £1.5-million loan secured against it were not paid.

The news that *Flying Scotsman* might be sold to recover the Plc's debts raised fears that the locomotive might be sold abroad. Now there were no illusions: only someone very wealthy could afford to run such a machine – and there was also the possibility that it might be placed on static display, never to turn a wheel again. Would-be owners came out of the woodwork, and in December 2003 two parties were thought to be interested if the locomotive did become available for purchase. The inevitable happened and *Flying Scotsman* was put on the market for sale to the highest bidder. The reserve was £2 million: Gresley would have been astonished.

Chapter Sixteen
Save Our Scotsman

*F*lying Scotsman has always sparked debate and interest, but never more so than when she came on the market following the collapse of Flying Scotsman Plc in early 2004. The locomotive was the Plc's main asset, and was expected to command prices that looked extortionate. One car auctioneer connected with the sale talked of the engine achieving an £8 million sale price – more than eight times the price expected for a similar-sized 'Pacific' locomotive, and a figure that would build at least three new A3s according to one magazine!

What was responsible for the current situation and the possibility of *Flying Scotsman*'s sale was the financial burden of operating the locomotive – coupled with Flying Scotsman Plc's massive debts accrued through the failure of the Edinburgh village concept. The Plc's accounts showed a loss of £474,619 in 2002 on a turnover of just £238,102, not helped by *Flying Scotsman* having missed booked work worth £48,000. The losses were blamed on delays in completing the proposed Flying Scotsman Village in Edinburgh, but that wasn't all. Although the project had put a financial burden on the company, the underperformance of the £2.2-million share issue launched in 2002 didn't help either. In any case, the Village, which was to be the answer to all the Plc's financial problems, never materialised, and as time went on fears for *Scotsman*'s future soon became big news in the railway press. The locomotive faced her most uncertain future since she had become stuck in America in 1972.

First came the revelation that she was being touted for sale by classic car dealer Malcolm Elder. He had overseas contacts, and very quickly the possibility of *Flying Scotsman* being sold abroad became a real concern. Initially the possibility of auctioning 4472 was denied by Flying Scotsman Plc Chairman Peter Shea, but the valuation estimates had already been made, ranging from a few hundred thousand pounds to the £8 million mentioned earlier. In February 2004 debt agency GVA Grimley made *Flying Scotsman* officially available for sale on behalf of Flying Scotsman Plc, via a sealed-bid auction. The floor was open to anyone, and until the new owner was revealed in April, no one could know who the new owner of this most famous steam locomotive would be.

Back in 1996 Marchington had paid the highest price ever known for a steam locomotive when he purchased *Flying Scotsman* and five coaches for around £1.3 million. Big locomotives will always attract a premium, and the fact that it is usually a once-in-a-lifetime chance to buy such a machine bumps up any possible sale price even further. Very few steam locomotives have changed ownership since entering preservation, although music mogul Pete Waterman and London businessman Jeremy Hosking have purchased several locomotives each to build up impressive individual collections. (Hosking had bought Marchington's Gresley A4 60019 *Bittern* in 2000, another asset sold to support *Flying*

Scotsman, and his name would be heard again when it came to the sale of 4472.)

Barclays Bank wanted to recoup the £1.2-million overdraft which the Plc had racked up, and, even though some commentators believed the locomotive was really, in physical terms, worth around £500,000 to £750,000, the final sale price was still estimated at between £1 million and £2 million. A quick sale was wanted, and, even though the sale was only announced in February, the deadline was just six weeks away on 2 April.

Within days of *Flying Scotsman*'s sale being announced the whole of the UK and much of the western world would hear of her plight. The railway press went into overdrive, as news of the sale filled the pages and her picture even graced the covers on several occasions. Her status as a British icon took her into the daily papers, and she is known to have appeared in at least one American newspaper, the *New York Times*, around the time of the sale.

As the news rippled through the railway world, interest began to bubble, but at the time no one quite realised the significance of a particularly prescient comment National Railway Museum Head Andrew Scott had made some time before. In *Steam Railway* magazine in October 2003 he said: 'I'm very clear that the future of the locomotive is in operation, and the heritage railway movement must find a way to achieve that, whilst at the same time achieving stable ownership for the locomotive.'

It was a worrying time for *Flying Scotsman*'s future: she could be stuffed and mounted on a plinth, never to steam again; or worse still, she could be sold abroad. Fears subsided a little at the thought that, in theory, export law prevented *Flying Scotsman* leaving the country. Then it was realised that, if an overseas bidder was successful in securing *Flying Scotsman*, the locomotive might not be allowed to leave the country straight away: six months would be allowed for a UK counter-bid to be prepared. Time was short, and very quickly bidders started to marshal support.

Several private buyers made their interest in the locomotive clear to the auctioneers, among them private businessman Jeremy Hosking, and a group led by former National Railway Museum (NRM) head Andrew Dow. The latter wished to set up a trust to look after the future of *Flying Scotsman* and even went as far as to begin negotiations with the Heritage Lottery Fund and plan for a public appeal. At the time Dow said: 'I think it is clear by now that Scotsman can never have a future in private hands. The situation has clearly got to change.'

On the other hand, Hosking was reported to be weighing up his options over *Flying Scotsman*. He already had a substantial collection of locomotives, with at least four going through major restoration or overhaul. On top of the rebuild of *Bittern*, he was also having SR 'West Country' 34046 *Braunton* restored, had recently bought a GWR heavy freight tank (4270) and already had GWR 'Hall' 6960 *Raveningham Hall* in traffic at the Gloucestershire and Warwickshire Railway. But even Hosking wasn't sure whether *Flying Scotsman* should remain in private hands. Talking to *Steam Railway* magazine in March 2004 he said:

I genuinely haven't decided if I'm going to bid. I'm very interested to know what the railway community thinks about the locomotive being owned by the NRM. Most of us are concerned about *Flying Scotsman* and want what is best for it. With the NRM determined to bid and getting the support of the Heritage Lottery Fund, it makes the whole question of whether to bid a complicated issue.

That sentiment was echoed throughout the preservation movement, and at the top of the chain the National Railway Museum also began to take interest, since there was a public desire for this famous machine to become part of its collection. But, even with its support from the steam preservation movement, the National Railway Museum would never be handed *Flying Scotsman* on a plate. It would have to pay for it, just like any other bidder – and there lay the biggest problem.

While it was a large organisation, the NRM didn't have the cash to part with the minimum £1.5 million needed to have a chance of winning a closed bid for *Scotsman*. But what it did have was a huge amount of support from railway enthusiasts and, most importantly, the general public. When the sale was announced NRM Head Andrew Scott was in Japan with the Head of Knowledge and Collections Helen Ashby to attend a conference on railway conservation and visit the NRM's two partner museums. Scott received the news quickly, by email: 'We knew we would have to work quite hard to make a workable bid, and we contacted York to let them know that we would be going ahead,' he said.

Scott wasn't surprised by the situation: 'I think we'd not been convinced that Flying Scotsman Plc's business plan was sustainable for some time. I know I wasn't the only one who wondered whether it was deliverable. There was a definite feeling that things would come to a head.' So in anticipation of this situation Scott and the NRM had had quiet talks with the National Heritage Memorial Fund – a body dedicated to ensuring important British artefacts are saved for the nation – to sound them out about the likelihood of winning funds, should a rescue bid for *Flying Scotsman* be necessary. The fund gave them a clear steer in the affirmative.

Although anyone who wanted to secure this most famous of steam locomotives had to act quickly, the NRM also had to think carefully about how *Flying Scotsman* would fit in with its collection. On his return to York, therefore, Scott began discussions about the appropriateness of her joining the National Collection. Many had mourned the fact that 4472 wasn't selected for the National Collection by the British Transport Commission back in 1963, when she was withdrawn, but they were thankful that Alan Pegler had stepped in to save the day; now it was someone else's turn. Scott's mind was clear:

It would be nice to think you could plan a national collection, but in the real world you never have a clean sheet of paper, and you never know what's going to be important in the future. Stuff, as they say, happens.

You could construct a technical argument about the A4 – the record-breaking 4468 *Mallard* preserved in the 1960s –

being effectively an A3 GT, but nobody could argue that *Flying Scotsman* doesn't deserve a place in the museum on a historical basis: the story of *Flying Scotsman* is the story of the railways.

Moreover, although the National Railway Museum was now actively planning a rescue bid, it came as a surprise to many that it didn't already own *Flying Scotsman*. 'In most museums,' observed Scott, 'the most popular question is, "Where's the loos?". In the NRM, it's followed by "Where's *Flying Scotsman*?"'

At the time it seemed as if a number of nationally important icons were being put up for sale. Just before the sale of *Flying Scotsman*, an important Raphael painting was put up for auction for £11 million. It actually sold for around £20 million, half of which was funded by the National Heritage Memorial Fund. Comparing *Scotsman* with art, Scott explained: 'There wasn't much debate about *Flying Scotsman*'s importance. Take the National Gallery: you don't go for one Raphael; when a second one comes up you'd happily add it to your collection.' The comparisons between the exquisite engineering art of Gresley's A3 and A4 Pacifics is apt – and the chance to complete the collection of Pacifics couldn't have been passed up.

The NRM had an opportunity with a public appeal, and that is just what they did – with only six weeks to raise the massive target of more than £1.5 million needed to be in with a chance of saving *Flying Scotsman* for the nation. Simultaneously the people of Britain had a unique opportunity: a once-in-a-lifetime chance to do what thousands had talked about over the past decades – save *Flying Scotsman* for the nation and give her a home suited to her iconic status in the National Collection.

Scott and his colleagues at the NRM had made their position clear: if the opportunity arose, the museum would take custodianship of *Flying Scotsman*. He pledged to give the locomotive a working future and make her accessible to as many people in the country as possible. Elsewhere in the steam movement, former BR Special Trains Manager and *Flying Scotsman* Operations Director David Ward had a similar, but slightly different take on things. Looking back on the hard work put in by Roland Kennington and his team of volunteers to keep *Flying Scotsman* running, he said: 'The best reward for Roland and the team would be for the NRM to obtain ownership, set up an operating company and continue to make the main-line base in the London area.'

All this was up for discussion, but first the NRM had to prepare its bid. A final decision from the National Heritage Memorial Fund was expected in late March, but that still left a major shortfall – because, in order to secure potentially ninety per cent of the funding from the NHMF, the NRM first had to raise the remaining ten per cent.

The National Railway Museum's marketing department had the task of telling the nation about the campaign that became known as SOS – Save Our Scotsman. The effect was massive. Television news programmes cottoned on, and the daily papers – both national and local – took up the story and told millions of Britons that the National Railway Museum had launched an appeal to save one of the world's most famous steam locomotives. The appeal itself was then launched in a blaze of glory in York in co-operation with the LNER's train operator successor, GNER. A sustained burst of publicity highlighted the engine's situation and warned that she could be sold abroad. This struck a chord with the public, whose heartstrings had been pulled by the thought of losing *Flying Scotsman*: the game was on.

Even though initial publicity had been favourable, there was no guarantee that a public appeal would be successful. The Save Our Scotsman team had to keep up the momentum and wait for the public to give their verdict. The millionaire entrepreneur Richard Branson provided a lifeline by offering to match the public's donations pound for pound, and his support came at a crucial time. His Virgin company ran the West Coast Main Line's long-distance trains, and his high public profile guaranteed more publicity. His motivation to support the campaign had little to do with his train companies, though: 'The big chequebooks of American museums have taken too many wonderful things away from Britain, and that's why we decided to intervene and keep it here,' he said. Not long before, Virgin Atlantic had missed out on a bold bid to keep the iconic aircraft *Concorde* flying. This time he was determined to keep this British icon running.

Branson's generosity was boosted by good news from the National Heritage Memorial Fund, which granted £1.8 million towards the engine's purchase, but, even so, more support was still needed. 'We had a few short weeks to raise an awful lot of money, and had to hit the ground running with the marketing,' recalls Camilla Harrison, one of the key organisers of the appeal. 'The *Yorkshire Post* was a very high-profile backer of the Save Our Scotsman campaign, and national media coverage was phenomenal.' A press conference at *Flying Scotsman*'s Southall base to highlight the locomotive's situation also proved to be a real turning point, as it gave the NRM access to national and international media (who, despite their protestations to the contrary, generally prefer to cover stories close to their bases in the capital). That placed the appeal on the national agenda, which in turn lifted the profile to a national and international appeal.

The money was starting to come together. Yorkshire Forward came up with a grant for around £500,000, and by now, with Branson's generous offer to match the public's donations, money was coming in fast through the public appeal. Response to the Museum's campaign really was exceptional: never before had any railway locomotive attracted so much attention from people of so many different backgrounds. Children of all ages donated their change, adults who would have never seen the locomotive in service and who had little interest in railway preservation found money to donate, whilst a few individuals with the money and a specific interest in seeing *Flying Scotsman* saved for the nation dug deep into their pockets and added sizeable sums to the fund. In less than a month the appeal drew 6,000 individual donations totalling £365,000 and ranging from £1 to £50,000. Andrew Scott almost found it overwhelming: 'It was the most amazing thing seeing this avalanche of paper come in every morning.' The Friends of the National Railway Museum joined in, pledging £25,000, and railway journals, notably *The Railway Magazine*, *Steam Railway*, and *Heritage Railway* all urged their readers to support the bid. Saving *Flying Scotsman* for the nation became a national campaign, and wherever you were in the country you couldn't fail to hear about the museum's appeal.

As the deadline loomed, there was still uncertainty about whether the funds raised by the NRM would be enough. It was known that railway enthusiast and London businessman Jeremy Hosking was interested in *Flying Scotsman* to run in Britain, but there was also still talk of foreign buyers. At one stage the auctioneers stated that there could be around fifteen serious bidders interested in the apple-green icon, though only the National Railway Museum had made its intentions publicly known.

As the deadline of 2 April approached the tension became almost palpable in York. The NRM's brilliant emotive, sustained, and assertive campaign had secured funding of £3 million for the locomotive (it was always intended that any surplus should go towards funding an exhibition dedicated to this icon). But sealed bids meant it was impossible before the deadline to find out if this was enough. With so many bidders having been rumoured to be in the running earlier in the NRM's campaign, there was a chance *Scotsman* could stay in private hands.

The NRM had a bid of £2.2 million ready, but had to sit and wait patiently for 2 April, when bids were finally submitted. It took three long days for the winner to be announced. Seven bidders had put in offers for *Flying Scotsman* starting at £600,000, around the accepted value of a locomotive of similar size. If there were any foreign bids, they were disappointed, because on 5 April, Scott, the National Railway Museum and the public got the news that they had been so hoping for: the public bid for *Flying Scotsman* had been chosen. After decades of being 'the people's engine' in everyone's heart, she was finally the people's engine in every sense. Andrew Scott sent an email to all the NRM staff congratulating them on their efforts. He also let them know the acquisition would have a profound impact on the future of the museum. 'This acquisition is completely different to everything else, and it will change the museum completely,' he said.

Flying Scotsman's future was now secure. The sale price had even included the spare A4 boiler, a spare cylinder from former classmate 60041 *Salmon Trout* and other useful goodies, and, what is more, the NRM even had some spare money to finance the engine's operation. In the final analysis, the fund amounted to £365,000 donated by the public and matched by Sir Richard Branson, £1.8 million from the NHMF and £600,000 from Yorkshire Forward. Those anticipating an immediate return to traffic would be disappointed as there were some mechanical issues to resolve, but after so long in private ownership *Flying Scotsman* was now safe, and would be safe for the nation to marvel at for years to come.

Flying Scotsman Plc Chief Executive Peter Butler, while

presumably relieved that the sale was completed with little controversy, issued a statement, saying:

> I am pleased that this icon of British engineering will now be in the National Collection. I look forward to seeing her out on the main line for many years to come.
>
> Private owners and Flying Scotsman Plc have run her for 41 years and she has done us all proud. We hand her over in better condition than she was last in public ownership, and we wish her well.

Everyone, it seemed, was delighted.

Following the sale, the Plc was able to complete the business end of the deal. Barclays Bank received around £1.5 million to settle the overdraft, leaving an additional £700,000 which was used partly to pay off creditors, ending the company's financial roller coaster and putting it back into the black – but this time without *Flying Scotsman* under its wing.

Forty-one years earlier, when she was withdrawn from BR service, Alan Pegler had saved *Flying Scotsman* from the cutter's torch with just a few weeks' notice for interested parties to raise funds. He was overjoyed with the news saying: 'Everything has come out exactly as I hoped.' He added, 'I was so damned excited after I heard the news that I hardly slept, and I was up at the crack of dawn to hear the first BBC news bulletin at 6.10 am.'

Chapter Seventeen
In Public Hands

The whole country was pleased that *Flying Scotsman* was now in public ownership and that a bright future now beckoned. Instantly the NRM announced plans to make her the central attraction at its major nine-day 'Railfest' event to celebrate 200 years since the building of the first successful steam locomotive back in 1804. With the public in mind, and the huge number of donations it had contributed, the NRM followed up its pledge to make *Flying Scotsman* accessible to everyone by planning a series of budget-priced York-to-Scarborough trains to take day trippers from the NRM's home to the east coast town.

Her new circumstances offered *Flying Scotsman* a slightly more sedate pace of life, for hauling trains along the easily graded York–Scarborough route was less taxing than being thrust into front-line duty at the head of the 600-tonne VSOE dining trains – no mean feat for any big steam locomotive. Some thought this a waste of a powerful engine, but the NRM, while wanting to keep *Flying Scotsman* in operational condition, also had a duty to look after the best interests of this 81-year-old lady. Any plans to send her to heritage railways were hampered by the fact that she was now only equipped with air-braking – vacuum brake equipment having been removed during her last overhaul. This meant that, in her current state, the only place to make use of *Flying Scotsman* was on the main line: a difficult and expensive task, but the NRM was keen to stress that 4472 would continue to be used.

She had already put in an impressive 32,000 miles' service for VSOE during her three-and-a-half years as the main engine for its prestigious dining trains. Indeed, when *Flying Scotsman* became part of the National Collection she was midway through a contract with VSOE, and there were still twenty trains booked for her to haul from London termini to destinations across the south of England. However, the contract with VSOE wasn't part of the sale deal, so VSOE had to find locomotives from elsewhere in preservation, including Bulleid air-smoothed 'Battle of Britain' 34067 *Tangmere* and rebuilt classmate 34027 *Taw Valley*.

Life on the main line is hard work for those who operate locomotives like *Flying Scotsman*. Conditions for main-line steam operation have become more stringent as time has passed and technology has advanced. New safety equipment called Train Protection Warning System (TPWS) was introduced as an industry-standard safety device following a major train crash at Ladbroke Grove in 1999 which involved one train passing a signal at danger colliding head on with another train travelling in the opposite direction. This devastating accident shook the whole railway system and was felt by all the main-line train operating companies and the preservation movement too. Safety had for many years been the railways' number-one priority, and needed to be paramount.

The introduction of TPWS – an electronic device that applies the brakes if a train approaches a red signal too fast – caused a new problem for steam locomotive operators, because now, on top of the expense of overhauling or restoring a locomotive, there was an additional bill for the best part of £30,000 to install TPWS. This put a strain on several locomotive owners, some to the point that they had to resign themselves to operating only on preserved railways, with their maximum speed of 25mph. For locomotives like *Flying Scotsman*, however, running on preserved lines wasn't an option, and under the ownership of Flying Scotsman Plc she had been fitted with TPWS during the summer of 2003, well ahead of the final deadline for its introduction of 1 January 2004.

Even though *Flying Scotsman* had been maintained and operated professionally, when it came into NRM ownership there were some teething troubles, and none more public than those that spoiled her debut appearance after the sale at the NRM's major nine-day festival Railfest. Completion of the sale had come during the final run-up to the event, and the NRM wanted to mark the locomotive's homecoming at the opening ceremony. It had planned a special VIP train to run from Doncaster to York hauled by its new acquisition, but preparations the evening before the run at Doncaster revealed several leaking boiler tubes, which prevented the Pacific from running safely at the head of a train. That meant *Flying Scotsman* wouldn't pass a fitness to run examination – carried out before every main-line run performed by any railway locomotive. In a hasty change of plan *Flying Scotsman* was towed from Doncaster to York by a diesel locomotive ready for the next day, whilst main-line steam operator West Coast Railway brought in its GWR 'Hall' 5972 *Olton Hall*, which itself was now famous for its appearances in red livery as 'Hogwarts Castle' in the Harry Potter films.

On the official opening day of Railfest, 29 May, *Flying Scotsman* was due to break through a banner under its own power, but in the event it was propelled through by former Royal Train Class 47 47798 *Prince William* – also now part of the National Collection. Thousands were there to witness *Flying Scotsman*'s return to national ownership, and nobody seemed to mind that on this occasion she wasn't running under her own power. The crowd was tightly packed, cameras were everywhere, and people strained to catch a glimpse of this awesome piece of British engineering history. Gresley would surely have been proud to witness such a moment: one of his locomotive designs, a combination of human skill and precision engineering, was now being treated more like a superstar than a railway locomotive. Bagpipes played as *Scotsman* burst through the banner to ecstatic cheers, but for the rest of the event she was on static display alongside other significant locomotives from railway history.

Following Railfest, *Flying Scotsman* was taken into the museum's workshops for urgent repairs to fit her for a return to active duty at the head of the planned series of summer trains between York and Scarborough which started on 20 July. The damage was worse than expected, though, and immediately after spending £2.2 million buying the

1923-built engine, the NRM had to fork out another £20,000 to replace every single small tube in the boiler, after the discovery of a split tube during an inspection. (The failed tube had been fitted during the engine's last overhaul in 1999 and had given five years' loyal service.)

The NRM called for tenders to retube *Flying Scotsman*. It was important for all those who had donated to the Save Our Scotsman Appeal that the engine was back in working order in time to fulfil its duties on the 42-mile York–Scarborough run in late July. The trains – called 'Ride the Legend' – were due to run on Tuesdays, Wednesdays and Thursdays, with two return trips planned each day. But there was more to it than that. This was the first real opportunity for several years for the public to travel behind *Flying Scotsman* (when it hauled the VSOE dining trains the price of tickets meant that only the well-off could afford to do so). It was essential that the ticket prices were fair and reasonable; they had to be budget prices, and the travellers had to get their money's worth. So the NRM was offering a return main-line train journey behind *Flying Scotsman* for just £25 per adult.

Steam engineering company LNWR Crewe – Pete Waterman's company – stepped up to the mark and completed the retube of *Flying Scotsman* by 6 July, and on 9 July the boiler was subjected to a hydraulic pressure test to check for any leaks. Its condition was satisfactory, so a steam test was booked for 12 July, and by 20 July – the first day of the special 'Ride the Legend' trains – a gleaming *Scotsman* was in steam and at the head of the first train.

One of the people involved with the Scarborough trips in

2004 and 2005 was the NRM's Tracey Parkinson, an enthusiast through and through and one with a soft spot for *Flying Scotsman*:

> I've known *Flying Scotsman* for a while. I met Roland Kennington a few years before I became involved with her here [at the NRM] and joined the support crew before she became part of the National Collection. I'd known *Flying Scotsman* on and off and already had a good rapport with the engine. Personally, I wasn't concerned with who owned it, so long as it was kept running – that was the important part to me.
>
> I hadn't prepared myself for how much this babe was in demand. 2004 was the first time for many years that the public could afford to ride behind *Flying Scotsman*. We ran 'Ride the Legend' three days a week for six weeks, making two return trips between York and Scarborough every day. Lunchtime trains were always full, but before we started running the trains only half of the tickets had sold. Once we were out there running, they sold out rapidly.

Flying Scotsman was starting to reach the point where a major overhaul was required again, and when the NRM bought her she was already five years through her ticket, and in need of some tender loving care. It surprised few that consistent reliability proved elusive, and on several occasions, other steam locomotives had to deputise. But the fact that *Flying Scotsman* was proving so erratic in public ownership is no criticism of Roland Kennington and the support crew who had tended her for many years: every ounce of Kennington's engineering brilliance had been used to keep *Flying Scotsman* running for the Plc, always on a shoestring, and often against the odds.

Running the trains from York was a busy operation. As Train Manager, Tracey Parkinson was responsible for a team of seventy volunteer stewards and had to deal with complaints, wrong tickets, passengers on the wrong train – they even had a lady travelling to Aberdeen who boarded *Flying Scotsman*'s train by mistake. Tracey recalls:

> We did have some battles with people getting on the wrong train, even though we were using much older carriages, and, of course, had *Flying Scotsman* at the front. This was made more difficult by the fact that we only had three minutes of platform time at York, because the station is so busy, so problems had to be resolved quickly.

Midway through the 2004 season came devastating news. Concerns were raised over the condition of an old repair to a crack in *Flying Scotsman*'s cylinders, and this led to talk of the engine being withdrawn a year early at the end of the first season of 'Ride the Legend' trains for a thorough two-year overhaul. The NRM had to consider the position carefully: it had a duty to care for the locomotive, but it also had the public, which had donated so much towards the purchase of *Flying Scotsman*, to think of too.

Flying Scotsman soldiered on through her six-week stint on the 'Ride the Legend' trains and suffered five mechanical failures which prevented her from hauling trains, including problems with steam pipes, leaking firebox stays and a superheater element popping out of its mounting. The machine herself wasn't running at full strength – she was tired from five years of hard work on the main line. All the same, the 'Ride the Legend' trains, even with a few failures, had done the museum proud. A total of around £400,000 in revenue was earned from the sale of 17,000 tickets, but, more importantly, the NRM had made a profit of £100,000 just a few months after buying the engine. This was a steep change in the fortunes of a locomotive which had been troubled by a lack of finance on several occasions. Already it was earning its keep and contributing to its own future. Good news indeed.

A programme of winter repairs was planned by NRM Rail Vehicle Collections Manager Jim Rees to prepare the locomotive for the 2005 season of 'Ride the Legend' trains on the same route as in 2004, but before that the apple-green Pacific had a prestigious train pencilled in for the autumn: a date with Prime Minister Tony Blair and the opening of the new NRM outpost at Shildon, 'Locomotion'. The trip to Shildon was a great opportunity to use such a well-known and respected steam locomotive. Tony Blair was due to perform the opening ceremony at Shildon and with *Flying Scotsman* hauling the train; it couldn't have been a better plan. Sadly it didn't come off, as more repairs were necessary before the locomotive could be used on the main line again. In the event, Stanier LMS 'Duchess' 6233 *Duchess of Sutherland* took *Flying Scotsman*'s place at the head of the prestigious train. Fortunately *Flying Scotsman* was made available for the opening of the £11-million Locomotion complex, but she had to be a static exhibit.

It had been a busy year at the National Railway Museum, but its efforts didn't go unnoticed. The Heritage Railway Association awards are an annual event, and the most coveted of all the awards is the Peter Manisty Award for Most Outstanding Contribution to Preservation. In a year that included saving *Flying Scotsman* for the nation: reviving GWR 'City' 3440 *City of Truro* to mark a hundred years since it reputedly became the first railway locomotive to hit 100mph, in 1904; putting on the impressive nine-day Railfest celebrations and opening the brand new Locomotion museum at Shildon, it is perhaps not surprising to hear that the NRM won the Peter Manisty Award. It was an honour well deserved.

In November, and back in the workshops, *Flying Scotsman* was being prepared for a return to steam in May 2005, ready for the next season of 'Ride the Legend' trips to Scarborough. A massive list of ninety repair jobs was drawn up by the Museum, ranging from welding up the crack in the cylinder and overhauling the lubrication system to replacing firebox crown stays and remachining the piston heads. It was a daunting list, but the success of the 2004 season must have been a great aid to getting the job done.

This time there were two halves to the programme of 'Ride the Legend' budget trips with *Flying Scotsman*. First the trains would run between 31 May and 2 June, then *Flying Scotsman* would be on display in the museum for three days from 3 July to 5 July. The main season would start on 5 July and run until 8 September: altogether a total of nine weeks, with the locomotive running three days a week. A massive effort by workshop staff and volunteers at York had *Flying Scotsman* back in one piece and ready for a trial run on 24 May. Seven days later she was standing in York station under the wonderful and original train shed roof waiting to depart with her first revenue-earning train of the year. Things started well, but, again, *Flying Scotsman*'s reliability proved problematic – she really needed a major overhaul.

In September she was only on display for the masses at Crewe Works' Open Weekend; almost 30,000 people visited the show and saw the apple-green A3 in close-up. The locomotive's final duties before retiring for her planned major overhaul were a series of sell-out specials operated by Tyseley-based Vintage Trains. As ever, *Flying Scotsman* was a massive draw, and it was fitting to see the engine hard at work right up to the point when it returned to York for the overhaul.

During the summer 23,000 passengers had enjoyed the ride to Scarborough behind *Flying Scotsman*, and the engine truly had been brought back to the people. But – just as she had been ten years before, when Dr Marchington bought her from Sir William McAlpine and Pete Waterman – she was now very weary and needed the full attention of the workshop staff at York to strip her to her component parts.

At the time of writing, the aim is to complete the current

overhaul in late 2007 or early 2008, ready for a full return to main-line activity in 2008. *Flying Scotsman* will remain based at York, but NRM Head of Knowledge and Collections Helen Ashby said that the plan was to provide a range of trips to take the apple-green legend to as many people as possible. There will be short-term loans to other areas, and, if vacuum brake equipment is reinstated, doubtless there will be visits to Britain's preserved railways too.

Andrew Scott warned that *Flying Scotsman*'s arrival would change the National Railway Museum, and Helen Ashby agrees:

> It does make a difference because it is a national icon. We do consider it differently to other items in the collection, because it has been rebuilt and operated.
>
> We are trying to conserve the engine's iconic status rather than the actual nuts and bolts. Some objects in the collection are so original, that we keep them like they are. With *Flying Scotsman* being so altered, it is worth keeping in working order.

A big new exhibition telling the story of *Flying Scotsman* and the train she is named after has been quickly and expertly assembled by the National Railway Museum, much of it (sadly not including Ken Issitt's account, which arrived too late to be included) drawn from memories stirred by the campaign. By expanding *Flying Scotsman*'s story to tell those of the men and women who worked with her and the train, and to explain the development of passenger services, the

NRM is keeping a now-dimming memory of the steam age well and truly alive. The interpretation is brilliant, and when *Flying Scotsman* returns to the museum in between her rail tour duties, she will truly be a star attraction.

Popular folklore has it that little of *Flying Scotsman* is left; indeed Helen Ashby believes there are almost no original components from 1923 in her. But that misses the point: in her shape, sounds and in her metal *Flying Scotsman* epitomises the steam age like nothing else. Operating steam loco-motives full-stop is becoming an increasingly expensive and demanding business, as age takes its toll, and skills become more scarce. With stringent safety devices now mandatory that could never have been envisaged when steam loco-motives were built, with the price of engineering rising, and with Britain's rail network becoming ever more congested, main-line steam – at least, main-line steam aimed at making a profit – is becoming harder and harder to justify. Now, just as in the 1960s, owning a big steam locomotive is the prerogative of wealthy businessmen and a few groups of supporters dedicated to their own particular locomotive.

Because so little of *Flying Scotsman* is original, the National Railway Museum has much more freedom to keep her running, make any modifications needed, and show her off than it does with any of its other steam locomotives. Something like Stirling No 1, one of *Flying Scotsman*'s Great Northern Railway predecessors, will never steam again, because to do so would be to destroy historically important material, but no such considerations apply to *Flying Scotsman*.

With her, the intention is to preserve for future generations the sight, sound, smell and spectacle of a big main-line steam locomotive at full cry, and in the National Railway Museum, Britain has an institution second to none that is well able to do so. It's crucial that it does. *Flying Scotsman* represents the gloss and glamour of a long-gone golden age, the power and might of the steam age, and the passion, dedication, brilliance and creativity of a long line of railwaymen and enthusiasts, like Gresley, Sparshatt and Townend, and Pegler, McAlpine, Marchington – and now, the public.

I thought when I started writing this book that I would be able to find some simple answers to why *Flying Scotsman* is so famous, but it seems that the highs and lows of this remarkable machine's life provide ample justification in themselves. From her construction, to the Wembley exhibition and then Sparshatt's marvellous sprint down Stoke Bank; the last-minute escape from the cutter's torch; the contrast with the embers of BR steam; the American adventure – and her consequent rescue and second life under Bill McAlpine: all of these facets have burnished the aura and cemented the legend.

But I don't think these explain completely why *Flying Scotsman* is so well-known and loved. I think a lot of it goes back to the LNER's inspired decision to give the locomotive such a heart-achingly evocative name, and then to produce some of the most brilliant and stylish marketing of her namesake train throughout the 1920s and 1930s. So good was this marketing, I think it created a cultural memory of such strength that, fifteen years after the LNER ceased to exist, so many thousands went to pay their last respects on her final run in public ownership.

The media has also played a part right from the very start. For a long time *Flying Scotsman* and her sister locomotives were just about the biggest passenger locomotives in Britain – a kind of national flagship of the railways – and they attracted great interest. And once steam was on the way out, *Flying Scotsman* became a good, slightly quirky story for the media to cover: after all, it's not every day that a famous steam locomotive departs to and returns from America and Australia!

So she became famous at least partly because she was so visible, on rail tours, in news stories, and of course, in train sets. Hornby has sold many thousands over the years that included *Flying Scotsman* – and sales are still strong after more than forty years! There must be something about her that encourages people who drove her on their 'OO' gauge model railway to go and see her in the flesh.

And then there's the Thomas the Tank Engine factor. Grown-up rail enthusiasts may pooh-pooh the fictional little tank engine, but the Reverend Awdry – who travelled on *Flying Scotsman*'s 1968 non-stop run to Edinburgh – really hit on something by anthropomorphising the steam locomotive with a face. His creativity summed up something enginemen and -women have long known: that each locomotive has a personality, and that there is something more wonderfully alive about a steam locomotive than any of man's other creations. It's difficult to look at any steam locomotive without unconsciously tracing an Awdry-style face on to the smokebox: it's as if they were designed to look like a giant metal animal. Gordon the Blue Engine is clearly based on *Flying Scotsman*'s design, and that's something I remember recognising as a child when I first saw *Flying Scotsman* in the 1980s: the Thomas influence is strong.

On top of that, Britain is inordinately proud of its engineering marvels: *Flying Scotsman,* the Spitfire, the E-Type Jag, *Concorde* . . . they all transcend the boundary between engineering and art in a way that little else can. Which other country could have produced such icons?

But there's more still: three wealthy men were stirred by a patriotic desire to keep *Flying Scotsman* running for the nation – often at great expense to themselves. That's why Alan Pegler bought her in the first place; why Sir William McAlpine rescued her from America, and why Marchington bought her too.

The three men are quite different characters: Pegler is the flamboyant showman, always trying to push the boundaries; McAlpine the understated and rational enthusiast who wants to share his passion in the best way possible, by keeping the locomotive running; and finally, Dr Marchington, a man who sacrificed almost everything in a bid to do what he felt was his duty – to keep *Flying Scotsman* on the main line and on the most prestigious trains. They all deserve our thanks and recognition for keeping *Flying Scotsman* steaming when they did, and for giving so much joy to so many people over so many years. All three are heroes – no question.

And there's a sense of the Flying Dutchman about *Flying*

Scotsman. For the past four decades, it's as if she's been roaming the rails waiting for the public to finally welcome her into the National Collection. She's tried to find homes at Market Overton, Carnforth and Southall, almost been stranded in America – and finally, she can now join her stablemates in her natural home, the National Railway Museum: no other exhibit can claim to have done so much to earn her place there, been so far and become so loved.

I know that I could make a rational case for any one of a number of locomotives – most notably *Caerphilly Castle* and *Duke of Gloucester* – as being more deserving of public adoration, but the love of steam, like any other love, is led by the heart, not the head. I started as a doubter, but in the process of writing her story, I've become yet another passionate admirer of *Flying Scotsman*.

She's achieved such incredible feats, been through so much, and despite repeated threats to her future, somehow she's always survived, and in the process she has become a kind of talisman for railway preservation, for steam and for the railway itself. If I had to choose a single locomotive to represent the age of steam, in its engineering, operation, marketing and social aspects 200 years hence, it'd be *Flying Scotsman* without question.

Flying Scotsman sums up the very best of British ingenuity, dedication, passion, bloody-mindedness and brilliance – and when she returns to the main line, she can roam the rails secure in the knowledge that she's finally come home to an adoring public: long may she continue to do so.

Acknowledgements

I'd like to acknowledge the help and assistance of a number of people, without whose efforts this book simply wouldn't have happened.

Firstly, I must thank my good friend and colleague Mike Wild, who has been a sounding board for the book from the start, and who generously stepped in to undertake some interviews at a time when I was unable to. His knowledge and expertise – particularly of the post-1996 period – have been crucial.

Others have been just as important. Nick Piggot, the editor of *The Railway Magazine*, has been an enthusiastic supporter of the book, and his interviews with Alan Pegler in particular – as well as his vast knowledge of everything to do with *Flying Scotsman* – must now be seen to be a vital part of the historical record.

Thanks also must go to the Hon. Sir William McAlpine, Bt (to give him his full title), who at very short notice made time in his schedule to invite Mike and me to his home and share his experiences of what it was like to own the most famous locomotive in the world.

The National Railway Museum has been marvellous, and hearty thanks must be offered to Andrew Scott, Helen Ashby, Bob Gwynne, Camilla Harrison, Tracey Parkinson,

Jon Pridmore and all the wonderful staff in the archives who pulled out the stops (and quite possibly some hair too) to share their material even when their whole archive was being reorganised.

Ken Issitt and Colin Churcher have been extremely generous with their time, sharing their experiences of life on the footplate and giving those of us too young to remember steam in the wild an appreciation of just how difficult – and, in Issitt's case, downright dangerous – their jobs could be. They, and all the other railwaymen and women in the book, are heroes.

Thanks, too, to the editor of that most esteemed of American rail enthusiast magazines *Trains*, Jim Wrinn, who put me in touch with a number of people who saw *Flying Scotsman* during its stay across the Pond.

To my partner Jenny – who has put up with hours of pacing the carpet, drafting sections of the book aloud – thank you for putting up with it. To my colleagues on *International Railway Journal*, thanks, too, for your forbearance.

To anyone whose contribution I've failed to acknowledge, please accept my sincere apologies: I have valued all contributions to the book, great and small.

Final thanks must go to my Publisher at Aurum Press, Graham Coster, Phoebe Clapham (who oversaw the early stages of the book), the managing editor, Nithya Rae, and the editor, John Wheelwright: their encouragement (even down to taking the Night Riviera sleeper to see me in Cornwall!) and support have been fantastic.

Bibliography

Books

Allen, C.J., *The Locomotive Exchanges 1870–1948*, Ian Allan Publishing, 1949

Brown, F.A.S., *Nigel Gresley: Locomotive Engineer*, Ian Allan Publishing, 1961

Cornwell, E.L. (ed.), *History of Railways*, Hamlyn, 1976

Dudley, John, *Flying Scotsman On Tour – Australia*, Chapmans, 1990

Hale, Don, *Mallard: How the 'Blue Streak' Broke the World Speed Record*, Aurum Press, 2005

Hughes, Geoffrey, *Flying Scotsman – The People's Engine*, Friends of the National Railway Museum Enterprises Ltd, 2005

Nock, O.S, *Speed Records on Britain's Railways: A Chronicle of the Steam Era*, David & Charles, 1971

Ransome-Wallis, P., *The Last Steam Locomotives of British Railways*, Guild Publishing, 1987

Sharpe, Brian, *Flying Scotsman – The Legend Lives On*, Mortons Media Group, 2005

Snell, J.B., *Early Railways*, Weidenfeld and Nicholson, 1964

Tuplin, W.A., *Great Western Steam*, Allen & Unwin, 1958
—— *British Steam Since 1900*, David & Charles, 1969

Unknown, *150 Years of British Steam*, Connoisseur Books, 1985

Whitehouse, Patrick and St John Thomas, David, *LNER 150: The London & North Eastern Railway: A Century and a Half of Progress*, David & Charles, 1989

Wolmar, Christian, *On the Wrong Line: How Ideology and Incompetence Wrecked Britain's Railways*, Aurum Press, 2005

Periodicals

Heritage Railway

LNER Magazine

Modern Railways

The Railway Magazine

Trains Illustrated

RAIL

Steam Railway

Videos

Flying Scotsman, the Most Famous Steam Locomotive, Tring International, 1995

Flying Scotsman Comes Home, True North Productions, 2004

4472 – Flying Scotsman, BBC, 1968

Index